Titles in the Jossey-Bass
5-Minute FUNdamentals Series

JOSSEY-BASS TEACHER

Jossey-Bass Teacher provides educators with practical knowledge and tools to create a positive and lifelong impact on student learning. We offer classroom-tested and research-based teaching resources for a variety of grade levels and subject areas. Whether you are an aspiring, new, or veteran teacher, we want to help you make every teaching day your best.

From ready-to-use classroom activities to the latest teaching framework, our value-packed books provide insightful, practical, and comprehensive materials on the topics that matter most to K–12 teachers. We hope to become your trusted source for the best ideas from the most experienced and respected experts in the field.

DEDICATION

To my teacher, colleague, and friend, Ira Finkel. I sat in your classroom and learned so much from your words and dedication to your profession. Then I learned even more about teaching from you as your Dowling College colleague. You were the best—the teacher that all students should have at least once in their lives, the fellow educator that we all truly admired. Thanks for your inspiration . . .

The GRAMMAR Teacher's Activity-a-Day

180 Ready-to-Use Lessons to Teach Grammar and Usage

Grades 5–12

Jack Umstatter

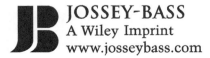
JOSSEY-BASS
A Wiley Imprint
www.josseybass.com

Published by Jossey-Bass
A Wiley Imprint
One Montgomery Street, Suite 1000 San Francisco, CA 94104-4594www.josseybass.com

Jossey-Bass books and products are available through most bookstores. To contact Jossey-Bass directly call our Customer Care Department within the U.S. at 800-956-7739, outside the U.S. at 317-572-3986, or fax 317-572-4002.

Jossey-Bass also publishes its books in a variety of electronic formats. Some content that appears in print may not be available in electronic books.

ISBN 978-0-470-54315-3

Printed in the United States of America

FIRST EDITION
PB Printing   SKY10030430_100821

THE AUTHOR

Jack Umstatter taught English on both the middle school and senior high school levels for thirty-five years. He also taught at Dowling College and Suffolk County Community College (New York). In 2006, he retired from the Cold Spring Harbor School District where he had co-chaired the English department.

Mr. Umstatter graduated from Manhattan College with a B.A. in English and completed his M.A. degree in English at Stony Brook University. He earned his educational administration degree at Long Island University.

Jack has been selected *Teacher of the Year* several times in his school district, was elected to *Who's Who Among America's Teachers*, and has also appeared in *Contemporary Authors*. A contributing writer for the *Biography Channel*, he now conducts teacher training workshops and performs demonstration lessons in classrooms across the country.

Mr. Umstatter's publications include *Hooked on Literature* (1994), *201 Ready-to-Use Word Games for the English Classroom* (1994), *Brain Games!* (1996), *Hooked On English!* (1997), the six-volume *Writing Skills Curriculum Library* (1999), *Grammar Grabbers!* (2000), *English Brainstormers!* (2002), *Words, Words, Words* (2003), *Readers at Risk* (2005), and *Got Grammar?* (2007), all published by Jossey-Bass/Wiley.

ACKNOWLEDGMENTS

I would like to thank the folks at Jossey-Bass, especially vice-president and publisher, Paul Foster, and editor, Margie McAneny, for their continued support, confidence, and guidance. Their assistance and friendship over the years has been invaluable.

I applaud and thank Diane Turso, my proofreader, for her meticulous work and careful review of this and other books that I have written.

Thanks to all my students, past and present, for making my teaching experiences both memorable and fulfilling.

As always, thanks to my wife, Chris, and my two daughters, Maureen and Kate, for their perpetual love and inspiration that mean so much.

ABOUT THIS BOOK

Contrary to what some out there are touting, grammar is not a lost art—nor should it be! Like the planet and the people who live on it, the English language is constantly evolving and changing. Some argue that this is for the better; some feel that it is not so healthy a change. Yet, the grammatical structure of the English language remains pretty much the same and has certainly not lost its importance. In fact, the constructors of local, state, national, college entrance exams, including the SAT Reasoning Test, the ACT, and even the Graduate Record Exam (used for graduate school admissions), have placed more emphasis on grammar and its components, as evidenced by the questions and tasks currently found on these highly regarded assessments.

Acknowledging the importance of grammar, usage, and mechanics on not only a student's academic profile, but also, and perhaps more significantly, on a student's ability to use language to communicate effectively and intelligently, *The Grammar Teacher's Activity-a-Day: 180 Ready-to-Use Lessons to Teach Grammar and Usage* was created to assist students to learn, exercise, and appreciate the many intriguing aspects of the English language. Though each of the 180 reproducible, ready-to-use lessons and activities that cover a wide range of grammatical components and more can be done within a short window of time, the long-lasting effects of these minutes will reap benefits for all of your students. These learners will speak more cogently, listen more astutely, and write more powerfully. Grammar will no longer be a foe, a force to be feared; instead, it will be an ally, a powerful friend who furnishes comfort and inspires confidence.

CONTENTS

Section Three   Mechanics • 145

Contents   **xiii**

Section Four   Show What You Know • 177

HOW TO USE THIS BOOK

The Grammar Teacher's Activity-a-Day: 180 Ready-to-Use Lessons to Teach Grammar and Usage is divided into four sections of reproducible grammar, usage, and mechanics pages.

The first section, Grammar, features 26 lessons and activities that cover the eight parts of speech in detail.

Usage, the second section, includes 114 lessons and activities. Here students will study important topics including sentence parts, phrases, clauses, sentence design and purpose, agreement, cases, and confusing and sound-alike words.

The 30 lessons and activities in the last major section, Mechanics, focus on punctuation, capitalization, and spelling, three essential elements of effective writing.

Show What You Know, the short, final section, serves as a check on what the students have studied. These 10 activities allow students to display their knowledge of all the topics covered within the book's pages.

Each of the 180 reproducible lessons and activities will take up only a few minutes of time in the already crowded curriculum that you and your students will cover during the year. If the pages inspire greater interest and discussion, go with it, for that is the desired teachable moment.

Use these pages as needed. They do not have to be done sequentially. So, if you need a lesson or an activity on commas, use the Table of Contents to select your specific need. Simply flip to the page(s), and you are ready to go.

You can use these pages for introduction, warm-up, review, reinforcement, remediation, or assessment. They are appropriate for whole class, small-group, or individualized instruction. Select what is most appropriate and beneficial for your students. An added plus is the Answer Key that will save you valuable time, a teacher's dream!

In short, the ready-to-use lessons and activities in *The Grammar Teacher's Activity-a-Day* will help your students improve their grammatical skills, enjoy learning about the English language, and gain confidence in the process. Isn't that what we all want for our students?

Jack Umstatter

SECTION ONE

Grammar

1 the noun

A **noun,** the first of the eight parts of speech, is the name of a person, place, thing, or idea.

person: Darlene, boy, mayor, worker, scientist, assistant

place: Los Angeles, dock, home, park

thing: automobile, tool, balloon, penguin, tree

idea: freedom, independence, enmity, thoughtfulness

A **singular noun** is the name of only one person, place, thing, or idea. Examples of singular nouns include *woman*, *auditorium*, *bicycle*, and *honesty*.

A **plural noun** is the name of more than one person, place, thing, or idea. Examples of plural nouns include *teammates*, *cities*, *houses*, and *freedoms*.

Activity

Underline the three nouns in each of the following sentences.

1. Rose carried her pet into the office.
2. The newspaper was left on the table in the classroom.
3. The group spent many hours discussing the new plan.
4. Joshua saw the bridge and the lighthouse.
5. Her computer was repaired by the technician on Tuesday.

Challenge

For each of these four letters, list four nouns, each having at least four letters.

b: _____   m: _____

_____   _____

_____   _____

_____   _____

g: _____   t: _____

_____   _____

_____   _____

_____   _____

2 types of nouns

A *noun* is the name of a person, place, thing, or idea. There are *singular* nouns that name ONE person (*player*), place (*room*), thing (*towel*), or idea (*love*), and there are *plural* nouns that are the names for MORE THAN ONE person (*players*), place (*rooms*), thing (*towels*), or idea (*loves*).

There are other types of nouns that are good to know. They include the following.

➲ **Common nouns** begin with a lowercase (or small) letter since they name *any* person, place, thing, or idea. They are nonspecific. Some singular common nouns include *actor* (person), *lounge* (place), *stick* (thing), and *kindness* (idea). Plural common nouns include *men* (persons), *headquarters* (places), *computers* (things), and *liberties* (ideas).

➲ **Proper nouns** begin with an uppercase (or capital) letter because they name specific persons, places, things, and ideas. Proper nouns include *President Harry Truman* (person), *Eiffel Tower* (place), *American Federation of Teachers* (thing), and *Theory of Relativity* (idea).

➲ **Concrete nouns** name a person, place, thing, or idea that can be perceived by one or more of your senses (seeing, hearing, touching, tasting, and smelling). *Popcorn, thunder, rainfall, skunk, windmill,* and *hair* are concrete nouns.

➲ **Abstract nouns** name an idea, feeling, quality, or trait. Examples of abstract nouns include *pity, weakness, humility,* and *elation.*

➲ **Collective nouns** name a group of people or things. Some collective nouns are *squad, assembly, team, jury, flock,* and *herd.*

3 the pronoun

The ***pronoun***, the second of the eight parts of speech, is a word that takes the place of a noun.

⊃ In the sentence, "Felipe is an intelligent student," the noun, *Felipe*, can be replaced by the singular pronoun *he*. Thus, the new sentence reads, "He is an intelligent student."

⊃ In the sentence, "We offered the baseball tickets to Rita and Drew," the nouns, *Rita* and *Drew*, can be replaced by the plural pronoun, *them*. The new sentence will now read, "We offered the baseball tickets to them."

There are several types of pronouns.

Personal pronouns refer to people, places, things, and ideas. *I, me, you, your, they, us,* and *it* are all personal pronouns.

Reflexive pronouns are formed by adding "-self" or "-selves" to certain personal pronouns. They "reflect" back to the person or thing mentioned in the sentence. *Myself, himself, herself, itself, yourself, yourselves,* and *themselves* are reflexive pronouns. There is no such word as *theirselves*.

Demonstrative pronouns can be singular or plural. They point out a specific person, place, or thing. *This, that, these,* and *those* are demonstrative pronouns.

Interrogative pronouns, like their name suggests, are used when asking a question. *Who, whom, which,* and *whose* are interrogative pronouns.

Indefinite pronouns do not refer to a specific person, place, or thing. Some indefinite pronouns are *another, both, everyone, most, no one,* and *several*.

4 personal pronouns

A *personal pronoun* refers to people, places, things, and ideas.

⊃ A ***first-person personal pronoun*** refers to the one (or ones) speaking. The singular first-person pronouns are *I, me, my,* and *mine.* The plural first-person personal pronouns are *we, our, ours,* and *us.*

> We told our story.
>
> I offered my opinion to the reporters.
>
> Ours is the less expensive model.
>
> The new family moved next door to us.

⊃ A ***second-person personal pronoun*** refers to the one (or ones) spoken to. The singular and plural second-person personal pronouns are the same three words—*you, your,* and *yours.*

> Can you bring your book back here today?
>
> The present will be given to you.
>
> This award is yours.

⊃ The ***third-person personal pronoun*** is the one (or ones) spoken about. The singular third-person personal pronouns include *he, his, him, she, her, hers, it,* and *its.* The plural third-person personal pronouns include *they, their, theirs,* and *them.*

> He and she wanted to take their children on a vacation.
>
> They asked him and her if the house had kept its appeal.
>
> Do you think that they will think that this car is theirs?

5 Do you know your personal pronouns?

Activity

Underline the appropriate personal pronoun in each of these fifteen sentences.

1. (We, Us) love to read books.

2. Most of these dresses had belonged to (her, hers).

3. (I, Me) will be waking up early tomorrow.

4. Emma has finished (her, mine) piano lesson.

5. Is this sweater (your, yours)?

6. You and (they, us) were invited to the graduation ceremony.

7. (Their, Theirs) is the cutest dog in this show.

8. Please pass the ball to (him, his).

9. Her grade is higher than (mine, him).

10. Does this instrument belong to (him, hers)?

11. (Our, Ours) car needs an inspection.

12. Were you able to hear (us, we) from that spot?

13. (We and they, Us and them) will meet at the movies.

14. Please help (they, us) lift this heavy box.

15. Listen to what (she, her) is telling (you, your) about the ship's cargo.

6 reflexive, demonstrative, and interrogative pronouns

A *reflexive pronoun* is formed by adding "-self" or "-selves" to a personal pronoun.

➲ **Reflexive pronouns** include the first-person pronouns, *myself* and *ourselves*. The second-person pronouns are *yourself* and *yourselves*. The third-person pronouns are *himself, herself, itself,* and *themselves.*

> The young lady carried in all her packages by <u>herself</u>.
>
> They relied upon <u>themselves</u> to finish the daunting task.
>
> Will he remember to help <u>himself</u> to the food on the table?

➲ **Demonstrative pronouns** point out a specific person, place, thing, or idea. *This, that, these,* and *those* are demonstrative pronouns.

> <u>This</u> birthday card is intriguing.
>
> <u>These</u> crossword puzzles sure are stumpers!
>
> Are <u>those</u> stars always visible to us?

➲ **Interrogative pronouns** introduce questions. *What, which, who, whom,* and *whose* are interrogative pronouns.

> <u>Whose</u> bicycle is this?
>
> <u>Which</u> of these is the correct answer, Paula?
>
> <u>Whom</u> did you ask to watch your dog while you went on vacation?

Activity

Underline the reflexive (REF), demonstrative (DEM), and interrogative (INT) pronouns in these sentences. Above each of those pronouns, indicate its type by using the three-letter code.

1. Who can learn this dance by herself?

2. Will you complete those problems by yourself?

3. Whom can I ask for help with these directions?

7 singular and plural nouns and pronouns

A **singular noun or pronoun** is a word that refers to *one* person, place, thing, or idea.

➲ Singular nouns include *car, desk, pool, friend, computer, video, geography,* and *poetry.*

➲ Singular pronouns include *he, she, it, I, me, mine, my, his,* and *her.*

A **plural noun or pronoun** refers to *more than one* person, place, thing, or idea.

➲ Plural nouns include *women, bottles, games, crafts, cylinders,* and *instruments.*

➲ Plural pronouns include *they, them, we, our, ours, their, theirs, themselves,* and *us.*

Activity

Write the letter S for singular or P for plural on the line next to each word.

1. _____ fan
2. _____ their
3. _____ ourselves
4. _____ licenses
5. _____ herself
6. _____ swimmer
7. _____ it
8. _____ bats
9. _____ graveyard
10. _____ few

11. _____ lights
12. _____ families
13. _____ I
14. _____ muscles
15. _____ gasoline
16. _____ myself
17. _____ them
18. _____ its
19. _____ we
20. _____ slide

8 the adjective

The **adjective,** the third of the eight parts of speech, modifies (qualifies or limits the meaning of) a noun or pronoun. An adjective can answer any one of these questions: *What kind? Which one? How many?* or *How much?*

In addition to *regular* adjectives such as *tall, muscular, beautiful,* and *intelligent,* there are two specific types of adjectives—the *proper adjective* and the *compound adjective.*

⊃ A **proper adjective** is formed from a proper noun. Examples of proper adjectives include *French* onion soup, the *Belgian* detective, *Orwellian* philosophy, and the *Kenyan* landscape.

⊃ A **compound adjective** is composed of two or more words. Examples include *part-time referee, eight-foot tree,* and *fifteen-year-old* musician.

⊃ *Note:* Do not hyphenate an adjective preceding an adverb that ends in *-ly.* Some of these instances are *smartly dressed* politician and *nicely groomed* model.

Activity

Write an appropriate adjective in each blank.

① Many of the _____ students voiced their displeasure with the new school rules.

② These _____ geese were searching for a _____ place to meet.

③ _____ and _____, the losing team did not look forward to their coach's speech.

④ Although the boss was _____, her _____ workers felt _____.

⑤ _____ people attended the play's _____ performance.

9 the noun-adjective-pronoun question

When is a specific word a noun? an adjective? a pronoun? Great questions!

⊃ Sometimes, a *noun* is used as an *adjective*. This is true for the word *garden* in the sentence, "The *garden* display attracted many visitors" since *garden* describes the type of display.

⊃ Examples of when a noun is a noun and when it acts as an adjective are found in the following sentences.

Joseph left his empty <u>glass</u> on the table. (noun)

Joseph left his cup on the <u>glass</u> table. (adjective)

The ball sailed through the <u>window</u>. (noun)

The ball sailed through the <u>window</u> pane. (adjective)

⊃ Sometimes, a *pronoun* is simply a pronoun. In other instances, it is an *adjective* and a *pronoun* at the same time and is then called a *pronoun-adjective*.

<u>Several</u> of the watches were expensive. (*Several* is simply a pronoun since it replaces the names of various watches.)

<u>Several</u> watches were expensive. (*Several* is a pronoun-adjective that describes the noun *watches*.)

<u>Many</u> of these computers were recently purchased. (*Many* is a pronoun that replaces the names of the computers.)

<u>Many</u> computers were recently purchased. (*Many* is a pronoun-adjective that describe the noun *computers*.)

<u>Some</u> of the roads were repaired. (pronoun only)

<u>Some</u> roads were repaired. (pronoun-adjective)

Activity

On a separate sheet of paper, write three additional examples of the noun-adjective-pronoun concept featured on this page.

10 the verb

The **verb,** the fourth of the eight parts of speech, is an action word. Since all good writing starts with strong verbs, this part of speech is very important.

The three basic types of verbs are the following:

➲ The **action verb** tells what action the sentence's subject (or doer) performs, is performing, has performed, or will perform.

Our lawyer <u>speaks</u> frequently with her clients.

This lawyer has <u>spoken</u> with some clients this week.

These attorneys will be <u>speaking</u> soon.

➲ The **linking verb** connects (or links) a subject (or doer) to a noun, pronoun, or adjective in the sentence. The words that follow a linking verb answer the question "*What?*"

Common linking verbs are *am, is, are, was, be, being, appear, grow, seem, smell, stay, taste, turn, sound, remain, look, feel*, and *become*.

These chickens <u>are</u> hungry.

Selena <u>is</u> the club president.

Note: To tell the difference between an *action* verb and a *linking* verb, substitute a form of the verb *be*. If the new sentence seems logical, the verb that you replaced is probably a *linking* verb.

Sylvia <u>sounded</u> the alarm. (action verb)

Sylvia <u>sounded</u> nervous. (linking verb)

➲ The **helping verb** assists the main verb in a sentence. One or more helping verbs can assist the main verb. If a sentence is a question, answer the question, and the helping verb will precede the main verb.

This mechanic <u>will</u> repair the auto this morning.

These mechanics <u>will be</u> inspecting the auto this afternoon.

<u>Has</u> the mechanic spoken with you yet?

11 Is it an action, linking, or helping verb?

Activity

Indicate the action verbs by writing **A** on the line before the sentence. Do the same for the linking verbs (**L**) and the helping verbs (**H**). There are at least three examples of each of these verbs within these fifteen sentences.

1. _____ Last night's audience members <u>seemed</u> more enthusiastic than tonight's audience members.

2. _____ Warren <u>is</u> going to ask his sister for some advice.

3. _____ <u>Can</u> you remember your teacher's first name?

4. _____ This talented surfer <u>rode</u> the wave all the way to the shore.

5. _____ Since Vicki had not eaten much today, her dinner <u>tasted</u> especially delicious.

6. _____ The doctor <u>examined</u> each patient twice.

7. _____ <u>Hustle</u> to first base, Charles!

8. _____ My niece quickly <u>grew</u> bored with the dull cartoon.

9. _____ Much of the required information will <u>be</u> reviewed during the three-week course.

10. _____ <u>Listen</u> to exactly what the director is telling you.

11. _____ <u>Hear</u> what I have to say.

12. _____ This <u>is</u> the correct answer.

13. _____ Greta <u>felt</u> tired after the grueling boot camp exercises.

14. _____ Each of these fifteen doctors <u>was</u> interviewed by the county health officials.

15. _____ <u>Will</u> you be able to help me move these books today?

12 the adverb

The **adverb,** the fifth part of speech, modifies (qualifies or limits) verbs, adjectives, or other adverbs. An adverb can answer any of these four questions—*Where? When? How? To what extent?*

⊃ **Adverbs modify verbs:**

Henry swam *brilliantly*. (*How* did Henry swim?)

The train *then* came down the line. (*When* did the train come down the line?)

The runner fell *down*. (*Where* did the runner fall?)

⊃ **Adverbs modify adjectives:**

The day was *almost* perfect. (*To what extent* was the day perfect?)

Some older people were *quite* happy with the club's proposal. (*How* happy were they?)

⊃ **Adverbs modify adverbs:**

Sonny, swallow your food *very* slowly. (*How* slowly should Sonny swallow his food?)

The architect worked *quite* methodically. (*How* methodically did the architect work?)

Though many adverbs end with *-ly,* these thirty-three adverbs below do not.

again	almost	alone	already	also
always	away	even	ever	here
just	later	never	not	now
nowhere	often	perhaps	quite	rather
seldom	so	sometimes	somewhat	somewhere
soon	then	there	today	too
very	yesterday	yet		

13 the preposition

The **preposition,** the sixth part of speech, is a word that shows the relationship between a noun (or a pronoun) and another word in the sentence.

Mollie walked *into* her aunt's house. (*Into* connects *walked* and *house*.)

My mom exercises quietly *in* the morning. (*In* connects the idea of *exercises* and *morning*.)

The professor placed the book *underneath* the large desk. (*Underneath* connects the idea of *placed* and *desk*.)

Note: To remember many of the one-word prepositions listed in the following box, remember the sentence, "The plane flew _____ the clouds." Any word that can be logically placed into that blank is a preposition. Then simply memorize those few that do not work in that sentence (*aboard, as, but, concerning, despite, during, except, like, of, out, since, till, until, with,* and *without*), and you will know your prepositions!

aboard	about	above	across
after	against	along	among
around	as	at	before
behind	below	beneath	beside
besides	between	beyond	but
by	concerning	despite	down
during	except	for	from
in	inside	into	like
near	of	off	on
onto	opposite	out	outside
over	past	since	through
throughout	till	to	toward
under	underneath	until	up
upon	with	within	without

14 compound prepositions and the preposition-adverb question

A **compound preposition** has the same function as the regular, one-word preposition. It connects a noun (or pronoun) to another word in the sentence. The sole difference with the compound preposition is that it contains more than one word!

according to	ahead of	apart from	as of
aside from	because of	by means of	in addition to
in back of	in front of	in place of	in spite of
instead of	in view of	next to	on account of
out of	prior to		

According to the author, this event happened in 1334.

We sat *next to* him.

In addition to the shed, we will also have to paint the basement floor.

We had a great time *in spite of* the nasty weather.

The Preposition-Adverb Question

The same word can be an adverb in one sentence and a preposition in another sentence. How do you tell the difference? Simple! Both an adverb and a preposition answer the same questions—*When? Where? How? To what extent?*—but only the adverb does it in a single word. The preposition needs other words to answer the same questions.

I walked *around*. (adverb) (*Where* did I walk? *around*)

I walked *around the block* (preposition). (*Where* did I walk? *around the block*)

The terrified dog scampered *past* (adverb). (*Where* did the dog scamper? *past*)

The terrified dog scampered *past us* (preposition). (*Where* did the dog scamper? *past us*)

Kenny, look *beyond* (adverb). (*Where* should Kenny look? *beyond*)

Kenny, look *beyond your present troubles* (preposition). (*Where* should Kenny look? *beyond his present troubles*)

15 the coordinating conjunction

The **conjunction,** the seventh part of speech, connects words or groups of words. In the sentence, "The video producer and the singer selected an interesting location for the shoot," the conjunction *and* connects the two nouns *producer* and *singer*. Similarly, in the sentence, "You can swim or jog during the afternoon class," the conjunction *or* joins the two verbs *swim* and *jog*.

A **coordinating conjunction** is a single connecting word. The seven coordinating conjunctions are *for, and, nor, but, or, yet,* and *so.* An easy way to remember these seven conjunctions is the acronym FANBOYS, in which the first letter of each conjunction is used.

Activity

Underline the coordinating conjunction in each of these sentences.

① I will not be able to go to the field for I have not completed my science project.

② Paola would like to be here with us, yet she has to watch over her younger sisters today.

③ This seems like a terrific plan, but I am not sure that the town can afford such a high tab.

④ Perhaps you or your neighbors will be able to organize the block party this year.

⑤ Do you think that we should put the paint on now so it will have time to dry?

16 the correlative conjunction

Just as the coordinating conjunction does, the **correlative conjunction** joins words or groups of words.

Here are the five pairs of correlative conjunctions.

Whether ... or   Either ... or
Neither ... nor   Not only ... but also
Both ... and

Note: Using only the first letter of the first word in each pair of correlative conjunctions, the mnemonic WNBEN will help you to remember these correlative conjunctions.

Whether the shark swims near the town beach *or* remains out at sea is the mayor's concern in the movie.

Neither the Olympics *nor* the World Series attracted the expected number of television viewers this year.

Emma likes to play *both* basketball *and* soccer.

You may select *either* the vacation *or* the car for your prize.

Not only will Desiree donate money to her favorite charity, *but* she will *also* volunteer at the group's annual fund-raiser.

 **Activity** Select a pair of correlative conjunctions to complete each sentence.

1. _____ the machine has been repaired _____ if it is still broken will affect our work schedule.

2. _____ the ventriloquist _____ the magician will accept our invitation to perform at the graduation party.

3. Marcelle enjoys playing with _____ dogs _____ cats.

4. The competent writer uses _____ poor word choice

   _____ vague details in her articles.

5. _____ will Olivia attend the meeting, _____

   she will _____ chair the proceedings.

17 the subordinating conjunction

The **subordinating conjunction** joins larger groups of words within sentences. It begins adverb clauses (groups of words that answer the questions *When? Where? How? To what extent?*). The subordinating conjunction can also be used to combine the ideas found in several sentences.

Here are the subordinating conjunctions, followed by sample sentences.

after	although	as	as far as	as if
as long as	as soon as	as though	because	before
even though	if	in order that	since	so that
than	though	unless	until	when
whenever	where	wherever	while	

Because Grandma was upset, she asked to be left by herself.

After Andy parked his new car, his sister asked for a ride.

The driver stopped her vehicle *where* the passengers were standing.

Our goalie, Caroline, looked *as if* she could block any shot.

We will probably have to finish *unless* you know someone who could do it for us.

Activity

Use a subordinating conjunction to complete each sentence. Use each conjunction only once.

1. We had not seen our old friends _____ they moved away several years ago.

2. These chimpanzees looked _____ they were displeased with the zookeeper.

3. Make the turn _____ you see the tall oak trees in front of the large white house.

4. "_____ you behave yourselves, you will not be able to go to the movies," Mom warned us.

5. I cannot stop from laughing _____ Garrett tells us his funny stories.

18 combining ideas with the subordinating conjunction

Activity

Use an appropriate subordinating conjunction to combine each pair of ideas or sentences. Insert punctuation where it is needed. Write your answers on a separate sheet of paper. Feel free to add or delete words, but keep the same ideas.

1. The bell rang. The students moved to the next period.

2. You finish your science project. You cannot play your video game.

3. We were watching the nightly news. We received a phone call from my aunt.

4. My cat, Belinda, started to hiss. The veterinarian approached my cat.

5. You will want to try an even harder puzzle. You solve a challenging puzzle.

6. I take your picture. Stand here.

7. Johann gets a ride. Johann will go to the concert.

8. François explored the surroundings. His friends asked him questions.

9. The garbage cans were left out in the street. The garbage collectors emptied the cans in the early morning.

10. Eduardo was pale. Eduardo saw a ghost. Eduardo is my brother.

19 the interjection

The **interjection,** the eighth part of speech, expresses strong emotions or feelings. Often found at the beginning of a sentence, an interjection is usually followed by either an exclamation mark (for strong emotions) or a comma (for mild emotions). An interjection can also be used to protest or command. Though interjections can stand alone, they are often contained within larger groups of words.

Wow! That was a close call. (strong emotion)

Oh, you are correct. (mild emotion)

Note: Good writers choose their interjections wisely for they know that too many interjections can decrease the writing's power and total effect.

Here is a list of the most common interjections.

aw	ahem	bravo	darn	dear me	eh
eek	gee	golly	goodness gracious	gosh	hello
hey	hi	hurrah	hurray	no	oh
oh no	oops	phew	psst	rats	ugh
whoa	wow	yea	yeh	yes	yippee

Activity   Write a sentence for each of these five interjections.

① gosh

_____

② oops

_____

③ yippee

_____

④ hurrah

_____

⑤ oh no

_____

20

20 parts-of-speech review (part one)

Activity

Identify each underlined word's part of speech. An answer can be used more than once. Use these abbreviations on the line before each sentence: n = noun; pro = pronoun; adj = adjective; v = verb; advb = adverb; prep = preposition; c = conjunction; and int = interjection.

1. _____ Each of the <u>programs</u> was taped.
2. _____ Joanna <u>programs</u> her television equipment.
3. _____ Fluffy, the family's cat, was looking down the <u>well</u>.
4. _____ I feel <u>well</u>.
5. _____ Dad bought <u>training</u> wheels for my brother's bicycle.
6. _____ <u>They</u> have been training at this site.
7. _____ <u>Hey!</u> Are you complaining about our group's meeting?
8. _____ All of the contestants <u>but</u> Monica were scheduled.
9. _____ These geese wanted to cross the street, <u>so</u> the tourists escorted them.
10. _____ We all helped to shovel the <u>snow</u>.
11. _____ Will it <u>snow</u> tomorrow?
12. _____ The <u>snow</u> shovel is out in the barn.
13. _____ The elderly man fell <u>down</u>.
14. _____ We chased him <u>down</u> the street, but we were unable to catch him.
15. _____ They made a <u>down</u> payment on a new car.
16. _____ The coach told Mitch to <u>down</u> the ball.
17. _____ The quarterback attempted a pass on the second <u>down</u>.
18. _____ Will you be able to move that large <u>box</u> by yourself?
19. _____ He <u>had</u> to solve the problem in a hurry.
20. _____ Uncle Erik gave Rick <u>box</u> seat tickets to the Yankees' game.

21 parts-of-speech review (part two)

Activity

Identify each underlined word's part of speech. An answer can be used more than once. Use these abbreviations on the line before each sentence: n = noun; pro = pronoun; adj = adjective; v = verb; advb = adverb; prep = preposition; c = conjunction; and int = interjection.

1. _____ Foolish <u>decisions</u> can cause trouble.

2. _____ She gained fame <u>quickly</u> as a journalist.

3. _____ You will <u>soon</u> know how difficult this is.

4. _____ Please <u>dispose</u> of your garbage.

5. _____ We can do this by <u>ourselves</u>.

6. _____ Tomas entered <u>into</u> the competition.

7. _____ Brianna <u>becomes</u> hysterical whenever she hears a funny joke.

8. _____ Rachel is an <u>heiress</u> to a large fortune.

9. _____ He <u>and</u> I can carry that bundle.

10. _____ You <u>or</u> they will be able to assist.

11. _____ The choir members walked <u>onto</u> the stage.

12. _____ Murphy is a <u>silly</u> dog some of the time.

13. _____ <u>Yippee</u>! I do not have to go to bed yet.

14. _____ <u>It</u> is my all-time favorite movie.

15. _____ Gary was <u>so</u> athletically talented that he was recruited by several colleges.

16. _____ This is the <u>story</u> of a seven-time award winner.

17. _____ Maurice is <u>preparing</u> for his lab experiment.

18. _____ The family room has been remodeled in a <u>modern</u> décor.

19. _____ I would love to attend the ceremony, <u>but</u> I already have another commitment.

20. _____ <u>Both</u> of these comedians will be appearing at local clubs this fall.

22 parts-of-speech parade

Use each word as indicated. Write your answers on a separate sheet of paper.

1. Use <u>part</u> as a noun.

2. Use <u>part</u> as a verb.

3. Use <u>televised</u> as a verb.

4. Use <u>televised</u> as an adjective.

5. Use <u>lower</u> as a verb.

6. Use <u>lower</u> as an adjective.

7. Use <u>for</u> as a conjunction.

8. Use <u>for</u> as a preposition.

9. Use <u>before</u> as a subordinating conjunction.

10. Use <u>before</u> as a preposition.

23 filling in the parts of speech

Activity

Fill in each blank with one word that logically fits the sentence's sense. Then, on the line preceding the sentence, write the word's part of speech using the code letters—noun (n), pronoun (pro), adjective (adj), verb (v), adverb (advb), preposition (prep), conjunction (c), and interjection (int).

① _____ A _____ mouse ran through our garage.

② _____ Either the doctor _____ the nurse will explain the procedure to you.

③ _____ Lucille is the gymnast _____ scored a perfect ten on the floor exercise.

④ _____ _____! That bicyclist almost crashed into the parked car.

⑤ _____ The brave soldier ran _____ the field during the skirmish.

⑥ _____ Creative writers entertain their readers quite _____.

⑦ _____ Two police officers _____ the building looking for the town officials.

⑧ _____ One of the most important _____ is found on that busy street.

⑨ _____ _____ of the guitar players stayed late to rehearse the number.

⑩ _____ _____ the barn we spotted several sheep.

⑪ _____ The machinist selected her tool from the _____ cabinet.

⑫ _____ Peanut butter _____ jelly is my cousin's lunch time treat.

⑬ _____ Take your _____ photo album to the party, Benny.

⑭ _____ The singing group was _____ into the Music Hall of Fame.

⑮ _____ It had rained _____ often lately that we cannot play our last scheduled game.

24 What's missing? (parts-of-speech review)

Activity

Insert a word in each blank. On the line before the sentence, write the inserted word's part of speech.

① _____ Christie had _____ shied away from a challenging situation.

② _____ Either Brian _____ Madeline will help you with these problems.

③ _____ Nobody can do all of this by _____.

④ _____ _____ several hours, many of us were very nervous after hearing the news.

⑤ _____ These _____ singers captured first place in the most recent contest.

⑥ _____ _____! You can fit that car into this small space?

⑦ _____ _____ Catherina sees that movie, she cries.

⑧ _____ Those talented _____ sold many of their stories to major publishers.

⑨ _____ Thursday _____ Marcia's favorite day of the week.

⑩ _____ The motorist drove _____ the long road.

⑪ _____ Helen's _____ actors were waiting for the director's advice.

⑫ _____ Our professor is very _____ and friendly.

⑬ _____ _____ is my favorite Canadian province.

⑭ _____ _____ you help the older woman with her situation?

⑮ _____ We think that she had _____ the record for the mile run.

25 fun with literary titles (parts-of-speech review)

Activity

Identify the part of speech of each underlined word in these literary titles.

1. _____ And Then There <u>Were</u> None
2. _____ The Taming <u>of</u> the Shrew
3. _____ Silent <u>Spring</u>
4. _____ The <u>Blue</u> Lagoon
5. _____ <u>Tender</u> Is the Night
6. _____ Thereby <u>Hangs</u> a Tale
7. _____ Romeo <u>and</u> Juliet
8. _____ The Cat <u>in</u> the Hat
9. _____ The Old Man and <u>the</u> Sea
10. _____ Writing About Your <u>Life</u>
11. _____ <u>Our</u> Town
12. _____ The <u>Chocolate</u> Wars
13. _____ <u>Arms</u> and the Man
14. _____ Far From the <u>Madding</u> Crowd
15. _____ Twelfth Night, <u>or</u> What You Will
16. _____ The <u>Adventures</u> of Huckleberry Finn
17. _____ A <u>Winter's</u> Tale
18. _____ <u>Anything</u> Goes
19. _____ The Hitchhiker's Guide <u>to</u> the Galaxy
20. _____ A Room <u>With</u> a View

26 parts-of-speech matching

Match the items in these two columns that deal with parts of speech. Each item in Column A is a word, suffix, or group of words. Write the correct letter from Column B on the line next to its corresponding number in Column A. Each answer is used only once.

Column A

1. _____ past
2. _____ activate
3. _____ specific
4. _____ calculated
5. _____ *-able*
6. _____ *-ion*
7. _____ *-ly*
8. _____ invent, invention, and inventive
9. _____ is, being, was
10. _____ snow
11. _____ during
12. _____ swift, swiftly, swiftness
13. _____ fleet
14. _____ whether
15. _____ aside from

Column B

A. a collective noun and an adjective

B. suffix used primarily for nouns

C. can be used as a noun, a verb, and an adjective

D. can be used as a noun, a preposition, or an adjective

E. a suffix used primarily for adjectives

F. a verb only

G. a compound preposition

H. a subordinating conjunction

I. suffix used for adverbs

J. a one-word preposition

K. an adjective

L. consecutively, a word's adjective, adverb, and noun forms

M. linking verbs

N. consecutively, a word's verb, noun, and adjective forms

O. an adjective and a past-tense verb

SECTION TWO

Usage

27 complete and simple subjects

⊃ The **complete subject** (the noun or pronoun that performs the action) contains all the words that help to identify the main person, place, thing, or idea in the sentence.

The complete subject in each sentence is italicized.

Many teachers and two principals from our school attended the musical concert.

Giraffes and monkeys in the local zoo captured the children's interest yesterday.

This novel's last few chapters are replete with great sensory language.

⊃ The **simple subject** is the main word within the complete subject.

The simple subject is italicized in each of these sentences.

This *taco* from the local store was quite tasty.

Some people never cease to amaze me.

These two *swimmers* graduated from the same high school.

Around the corner is the *local theater*.

 **Activity**   In each sentence, underline the complete subject and circle the simple subject.

① Threatening skies changed our picnic plans.

② Many engineers from neighboring communities have visited our sanitation plant over the last few years.

③ Huge trucks blocked our roadway for an hour during last week's terrible snowstorm.

④ The Padres will win the championship in our local softball league this season.

⑤ The talented actress signed autographs for thirty minutes after the play.

28 complete and simple predicates

⊃ A **complete predicate** is the main verb (action) along with all of its modifiers.

The complete predicate is italicized in these sentences.

Each of the seven contestants *will be flying to Los Angeles next week.*

The talented mechanic *fixed our car yesterday afternoon.*

My sister, a hairdresser, *studied hard for her state licensing examinations.*

Can you *recall his name?*

⊃ A **simple predicate (verb)** is the main word or phrase that tells something about the subject (doer) of the sentence.

The simple predicate is italicized in these sentences.

Izzy *roamed* the neighborhood last night.

The students *cheered* loudly for our lacrosse team.

Youngsters really *enjoy* that activity.

Will he *star* in the school play?

Activity

Underline the complete predicate and circle the simple predicate.

1. The citizens heard the blaring sirens.

2. Babies were crying during the awards ceremony.

3. Talented musicians give their best efforts all the time.

4. An angry bystander yelled at the speeding motorist.

5. Who will be chosen as this year's recipient?

29 compound subject and compound predicate

⊃ A ***compound subject*** is two or more subjects in a sentence. These subjects are joined by a conjunction and share the same verb. The compound subject is underlined in each sentence.

> <u>Happy</u>, <u>Sleepy</u>, and <u>Doc</u> knew Snow White.

> The <u>horses</u> and the <u>king's men</u> could not put Humpty Dumpty back together again.

> <u>She</u> and <u>I</u> will go to the dance tomorrow night.

⊃ A ***compound predicate (verb)*** is two or more verbs that are joined by a conjunction and share the same subject. The compound predicates are underlined in each sentence.

> An experienced pilot <u>studies</u> and <u>knows</u> about air currents.

> All of these cars were <u>made</u> and <u>sold</u> in our country.

> Hearing the exciting announcement, the audience members loudly <u>cheered</u> and <u>whistled</u>.

Note: In the sentence, "Renata <u>waxed</u> her car, and then she <u>parked</u> it in the garage," the two verbs *waxed* and *parked* are not compound predicates (or verbs) since they do not share the same subject. *Renata* and *she* (though the same person) are different subjects (in different parts of the same sentence).

Activity On a separate sheet of paper, use each pair of words as compound predicates or verbs.

1. walked, talked
2. ran, hid
3. earned, donated
4. remembered, responded
5. ran, threw, caught

30 the direct object

A **direct object** is a noun or pronoun that receives the action of a transitive verb (a verb that has an object) or shows the result of that action. A direct object answers the question "What?" or "Whom?" after the transitive verb.

In these sentences, the transitive verb is underlined, and the direct object is italicized.

My neighbor <u>asked</u> us an interesting *question*. (*What?*)

The television set <u>required</u> *repair*. (*What?*)

Tyler <u>edited</u> three *errors* in her essay. (*What?*)

They <u>oiled</u> the *skates* before lacing them up. (*What?*)

We <u>guided</u> *him* during the mountain climb. (*Whom?*)

James <u>met</u> *Mr. Hunt* in the school's main office. (*Whom?*)

Activity

Lucky Seven: Fill in the direct object with a word having these first and last letters and the total number of letter within the parentheses. The first one is done for you.

1. The man greeted his <u>brother</u> (7).

2. The baseball coach gave the man on base a s_____n (4).

3. This bee gave off a painful s_____g (5).

4. Pull the kite's s_____g (6).

5. Johnson, a reckless gambler, placed a large w_____r (5) on that horse.

6. Sylvia selected a b_____t (4) from the vegetable section of the supermarket.

7. Seymour found his old woolen s_____r (7) in the closet.

31 the indirect object

An **indirect object** is a noun, pronoun, or word group that answers the question "to whom?" or "for whom?" after the action verb. An indirect object precedes a direct object in the sentence.

In each sentence, the indirect object is italicized, and the direct object is underlined.

Mr. Higgins gave *Penny* an <u>award</u>. (*To whom* was the award given?—Penny)

Laura gave *us* a challenging <u>problem</u>. (*To whom* did Laura give the challenging problem?—us)

Their efforts earned *them* a handsome <u>reward</u>. (Earned a handsome reward *for whom*?—them)

Can Harold purchase his *mother* a new <u>home</u>? (Purchase a new home *for whom*?—his mother)

Note: Remember the difference between an indirect object and an object of the preposition.

The comedian told *her* a joke. (The indirect object is *her*, and the direct object is *joke*.)

The comedian told the joke to *her*. (The direct object is *joke*, and the object of the preposition is *her*. There is no indirect object.)

Activity

Circle the indirect object, and underline the direct object in each sentence.

1. Hillary's minister gave her a compliment.
2. Lance lent me some money to attend the concert.
3. Dad cooked Mom a delicious dinner last night.
4. Have they brought you the newspaper yet?
5. Will you please tell her the secret?

34

32 the object of the preposition

The ***object of the preposition*** is the noun or pronoun that follows a preposition and completes the prepositional phrase. The prepositional phrase can also include modifiers.

In the sentence, "The orange juice box was in the new refrigerator," the prepositional phrase is "in the new refrigerator." This phrase answers the question "*Where* (is the orange juice box)?" The object of the preposition is *refrigerator*. The modifier, or describer, is *new*.

The ***compound objects of the preposition*** are two or more objects, such as "Mom (and) Dad" in the sentence, "The party was paid for by *Mom* and *Dad*."

Activity

In each sentence below, underline the prepositional phrase, and circle the object of the preposition.

1. Our plans for the trip will need to change now.

2. We will need to change our plans for the occasion.

3. Unless the Grant family adds more space to their home, they will probably have to move.

4. Can you find your way home without me?

5. The picture sent from China is breathtaking.

6. Will Jermaine be willing to walk the dog after dinner?

7. This playground was built by community volunteers.

8. All of the puppets were bought immediately.

9. The puppets were sold by Christina and Carla.

10. Was he waiting long for you and Moe?

33 objects and 8-7-5

Twenty objects are underlined. There are eight direct objects (DO), seven indirect objects (IO), and five objects of the preposition (OP). Write the two-letter code on the line before each sentence.

1. _____ Two Navy officials award Hugo a <u>medal</u>.

2. _____ His physician told <u>Brian</u> the best way to lose weight.

3. _____ Sylvester gave his sister a gift during the <u>ceremony</u>.

4. _____ The cartoons on the large <u>screen</u> entertained us.

5. _____ All of the directors gave the young starlet good <u>suggestions</u>.

6. _____ Frank gave <u>Jim</u> a hard time.

7. _____ After his win, the racer celebrated with <u>friends</u>.

8. _____ Give Nancy your <u>bike</u> for this leg of the trip.

9. _____ The scientist brought the experiment's results to his <u>colleagues</u>.

10. _____ Patsy brought her friends more cold <u>lemonade</u>.

11. _____ Brad Lawrence, the hotel's owner, went to the <u>chiropractor</u> last Wednesday.

12. _____ Our principal, Mr. Hartill, taught <u>us</u> a valuable lesson.

13. _____ Ms. Bossi gave <u>Mr. Shierant</u> the keys to the gymnasium.

14. _____ Please bring the <u>book</u> back to Bobbie Brennan.

15. _____ Show <u>me</u> the correct method.

16. _____ Has Yvonne ever given her <u>sister</u> the secret that we share?

17. _____ Wilma walked <u>Dino</u> along the dusty path.

18. _____ They found the <u>situation</u> quite alarming.

19. _____ I showed <u>Christine</u> the city's new plans.

20. _____ Seth remembered the <u>answer</u> after his test had been collected.

34 subject complements— predicate nominatives and predicate adjectives

A **subject complement** is a word or group of words within the *complete predicate* that either identifies (with a *predicate nominative*) or describes (with a *predicate adjective*) the subject (doer of the action). There are two types of subject complements—the *predicate adjective* (the describer) and the *predicate nominative* (the identifier).

As an example, in the sentence, "*Our Town* is a play written by Thornton Wilder," the complete predicate, *is a play written by Thornton Wilder*, includes *play* (predicate nominative), the word that identifies what *Our Town* is. In the sentence, "The play was interesting and inspirational," the complete predicate, *was interesting and inspirational*, includes the words *interesting* and *inspirational* (two predicate adjectives) to describe what the play was.

The subject complement is underlined in these sentences.

O'Hare is a very busy <u>airport</u>. (predicate nominative)

Mike Smith is a terrific <u>friend</u>. (predicate nominative)

Indiana's capital city is <u>Indianapolis</u>. (predicate nominative)

She was the first <u>president</u> of that association. (predicate nominative)

Mitchell's report was factually <u>correct</u>. (predicate adjective)

The lake's water was crystal <u>clear</u>. (predicate adjective)

Gary's parents and grandparents are quite <u>successful</u> in the business world. (predicate adjective)

The basement was <u>moldy</u>, <u>dusty</u>, and <u>unpainted</u>. (predicate adjectives)

Activity

Fill in each blank with a predicate nominative or a predicate adjective.

1. My uncle's observations are generally _____.
2. Kathy's new car is _____.
3. Unfortunately, the movie was a(n) _____.
4. The name of our school's principal is _____.
5. The capital city of Wyoming is _____.

35 Predicate nominative, predicate adjective, or neither?

Activity

Five of the underlined words are predicate nominatives (PN); five are predicate adjectives (PA); and five are neither (NE). On the line before each sentence, write the two-letter code to indicate your answer.

1 _____ Elizabeth Bennet is her favorite literary <u>character</u>.

2 _____ She is very <u>agile</u> as a dancer.

3 _____ All of the musicians in the orchestra recalled their favorite <u>experiences</u>.

4 _____ The younger man is our new state <u>senator</u>.

5 _____ Last year's festival held in the state capital's fields was <u>fair</u>.

6 _____ These experienced carpenters displayed great <u>craftsmanship</u> over the last few months.

7 _____ The immediate effects of the new legislation are <u>widespread</u>.

8 _____ The message that he tried to interpret was <u>cryptic</u>.

9 _____ Today's weather conditions are <u>cold</u> and <u>rainy</u>.

10 _____ Monty and his buddies saw the <u>kayaks</u> in the store's large window.

11 _____ I had to meet my counselor, <u>Mr. Wilhelm</u>, after lunch.

12 _____ The most talented scientists in our school are <u>Tameka</u> and <u>Jose</u>.

13 _____ Tom L. Morgan is the <u>architect</u> in this photograph.

14 _____ We had never seen <u>them</u> perform before last night.

15 _____ This past drought was a huge <u>problem</u> for the farmers.

36 introducing phrases

A **phrase** is a related group of words that functions as a part of speech and does not contain both a subject and a verb.

⊃ **Verb phrases** do not contain a subject. Examples of verb phrases include *has been laughing, will remain,* and *does believe.*

⊃ **Prepositional phrases,** such as the adjective phrase and the adverb phrase, do not have a subject or a verb. Examples of prepositional phrases are *in the beginning, at the end,* and *after the trial.*

⊃ **Participial phrases** function as adjectives. In the sentence, "Walking home after the movie, Joe felt happy," the participial phrase is *Walking home after the movie,* and the participle is *Walking.*

⊃ **Gerund phrases** function as nouns. Gerund phrases can be used as subjects, predicate nominatives, direct objects, indirect objects, and objects of the preposition. In the sentence, "Walking home from the movies was a good time for Joe and his friends," the gerund phrase used as a subject is *Walking home from the movies.*

⊃ **Infinitive phrases** function as nouns, adjectives, or adverbs. In the sentence, "To beat the old record was Nina's goal," the infinitive phrase is *To beat the old record,* and the infinitive is *To beat.*

⊃ **Appositive phrases** describe or identify another noun or pronoun in the sentence. In the sentence, "Lake Harris, our favorite vacation spot, is off the beaten path," the appositive is *spot,* and the appositive phrase is *our favorite vacation spot.*

37 the verb phrase

A **verb phrase** is the main verb and one or more helping verbs.

Common helping verbs include these words in the box.

am	are	be	been	being	can		could	did	do
does	doing	had	has	have	having	is		may	might
must	shall	should	was	were	will	would			

The verb phrases are underlined in these sentences.

Many doctors <u>have been concerned</u> about the new flu.

Some of the new stamps <u>were purchased</u> by the collector.

The collector <u>had purchased</u> the new stamps.

We <u>had</u> never <u>witnessed</u> such a hysterical scene. (*Never* is an adverb modifying the main verb, *witnessed,* and is not part of the verb phrase.)

<u>Will</u> you <u>remember</u> my address and phone number? (*You* is the pronoun subject of the sentence and is not part of the verb phrase.)

<u>Is</u> Emma <u>practicing</u> her piano now? (*Emma* is the sentence's subject and is not part of the verb phrase.)

The runner <u>had</u> not <u>been passed</u> by any of the other contestants. (*Not* is an adverb and is not part of the verb phrase.)

Activity

Use each of the verb phrases in a sentence.

1 had been writing

_____

_____

2 will go

_____

_____

3 can be replaced

_____

_____

38 the prepositional phrase

A **prepositional phrase** begins with a preposition and usually ends with a noun or a pronoun.

The prepositional phrase is underlined in each sentence.

The elderly man went <u>to the doctor's office</u> today.

<u>In the morning</u>, the elementary school students perform their exercises.

These magicians performed many tricks <u>for the children</u>.

Tomas walked <u>into the dark house</u>.

The word that ends the prepositional phrase is the *object of the preposition*.

In each of these sentences, the prepositional phrases are underlined, and the objects of the preposition are italicized.

All <u>of the *trees*</u> had been pruned <u>by the *workers*</u>.

Someone <u>in this *office*</u> has borrowed the stapler <u>from *Markisha*</u>.

Will you show your necklace <u>to your *grandparents*</u>?

Activity

Underline the prepositional phrases and circle the object of the preposition in each of these ten sentences. There may be more than one prepositional phrase in the sentence.

1. She was lonesome without him.
2. They were jogging throughout the neighborhood.
3. Beyond the river is a beautiful park.
4. All of the sailors climbed aboard the ship.
5. In the meantime, please watch my backpack.
6. Therese had never seen such a sight in her backyard.
7. There was very little talk during the movie.
8. These men with their equipment are experts.
9. Some of the boats were moving along the river.
10. All of the women except Denise will be at the meeting.

39 the adjective phrase

An *adjective phrase* is a prepositional phrase that modifies a noun or a pronoun. This phrase answers the question *Which one?* The adjective phrase follows right after the noun or pronoun that it modifies or describes. Generally, if you *cannot* logically move the prepositional phrase within the sentence, it is most often an adjective phrase. Remember that an adjective phrase contains no verb.

The adjective phrases are underlined in these sentences.

Some programs at our local library were requested last year. (Which programs? *the ones in our local library*)

These women in this photograph are my aunts. (Which women? *the ones in the photograph*)

The programs on her favorite television station are often repeated. (Which programs? *the ones on her favorite television station*)

Activity

If the underlined prepositional phrase is an adjective phrase, write YES on the line before the sentence. If it is not, write NO.

1. _____ In the morning the cook prepares many different meals.

2. _____ The car in our driveway was recently purchased.

3. _____ These cameras near the office building are huge.

4. _____ We were more than happy with the new arrangements.

5. _____ Nicole has been traveling on many business trips lately.

40 the adverb phrase

A prepositional phrase that answers any of these questions—*When? Where? How? Why? Under what conditions?* or *To what degree?*—is an **adverb phrase.** If you *can* logically move the prepositional phrase within the sentence, it is probably an adverb phrase. Remember that an adverb phrase contains no verb.

The adverb phrases in these sentences are underlined.

We walked after dinner. (When?)

The little boys and girls ran into the hallway. (Where?)

Audrey, one of the chaperones, certainly handled herself with class yesterday. (How?)

John built the wooden shed with much assistance. (Under what conditions?)

The underdog candidate won the state election by a landslide. (To what degree?)

Activity

In each of these sentences, insert an adverb phrase that answers the question in the parentheses found after the sentence. Do not include any verbs within these adverb phrases!

1. The hilarious cartoon aired _____. (*When?*)

2. Wendy followed the older child _____. (*Where?*)

3. None of these young children could lift the heavy packages _____. (*How?*)

4. The championship boxing match was canceled _____. (*Why?*)

5. _____ we like to jog with our friends. (*When?*)

41 adjective and adverb phrases review

Activity

On the line before each sentence, write ADJ if the underlined prepositional phrase is an adjective phrase or ADVB if it is an adverb phrase.

1. _____ The magician <u>with his rabbit</u> entertained the crowd.
2. _____ <u>With the rabbit</u>, the magician entertained the crowd.
3. _____ <u>During the storm</u> we were quite frightened.
4. _____ The noise <u>during the storm</u> frightened us.
5. _____ Some information <u>in this book</u> helped me with my report.
6. _____ Sean left his pencil <u>in this book</u>.
7. _____ We found the missing coins <u>on the track</u>.
8. _____ The shoes <u>on the track</u> are Roberta's.
9. _____ The news program <u>at five o'clock</u> features local stories.
10. _____ We ate dinner <u>at five o'clock</u>.
11. _____ These planes directly <u>above us</u> are moving quite rapidly.
12. _____ The planes moved very fast <u>above us</u>.
13. _____ These plans <u>for the new recreation center</u> are fabulous!
14. _____ Much money was donated <u>for the new recreation center</u>.
15. _____ <u>In the taxi cab</u>, we had a heated conversation.
16. _____ Our conversation <u>in the taxi cab</u> was heated.
17. _____ The benches <u>in our backyard</u> are brand new.
18. _____ Dad moved the benches <u>into our backyard</u>.
19. _____ Have you met our new senator <u>from Vermont</u>?
20. _____ We are four hours away <u>from Vermont</u>.

42 prepositional phrases review

Activity

Underline the prepositional phrase in each sentence. Then write ADJ on the line before the sentence if the phrase is an adjective phrase or ADVB if it is an adverb phrase.

1. _____ The lawn was seeded today by the maintenance workers.
2. _____ We will open the museum's doors in a few minutes.
3. _____ Tickets to tomorrow night's concert will be sold starting this morning.
4. _____ There is a hint within every sentence.
5. _____ Several investigators asked us questions during their investigation.
6. _____ In fact, I do remember that funny incident.
7. _____ Water in this tank must be drained often.
8. _____ Without much fanfare the actress greeted her admiring fans.
9. _____ The student finished reading the book that was in her van.
10. _____ The Senior Citizens Center requested donations instead of something else.
11. _____ Barbara's bicycle with the basket should be moved soon.
12. _____ The view from Hester's living room is breathtaking.
13. _____ No lifeguard is on duty now.
14. _____ Such a wondrous event had not taken place near our house.
15. _____ Grab the rope with both hands.
16. _____ The buoy was bobbing in the bay.
17. _____ The buoys in the ocean were bobbing.
18. _____ We had waited for a very long time.
19. _____ Rachel's look of surprise confused us.
20. _____ The minister looked up into the heavens.

43 the appositive

An **appositive** is a noun or pronoun (often with modifiers) that is placed beside another noun or pronoun to explain or identify it. Essentially, an appositive is an additional word or group of words used to tell more about who (or what) that noun or pronoun is. No verb appears in an appositive phrase.

In each sentence below, the appositive phrase is underlined, and the appositive is italicized.

Michelle Rogers, the *lifeguard* at Smith's Beach, made three saves last month.

"The Ugly Duckling," Hans Christian Andersen's *story*, has entertained many children over the years.

My daughter's car, a *Toyota*, has certainly served her well.

The Little Red Deli, our neighborhood *store*, is more than seventy-five years old.

Eleven, Joe's house *number*, is also his uniform's number.

The cheetah, the fastest land *animal*, sprinted across the plains.

Marjorie Kinnan Rawlings, the famous *author*, won many writing awards.

Activity   Insert an appositive phrase into each of these five sentences. Remember that verbs are not included in appositives or appositive phrases.

1. I just finished reading my favorite book, _____.

2. Our class members recently visited Arizona's capital city, _____.

3. Barack Obama, _____, attended Harvard College.

4. December, _____, seems to go by very quickly each year.

5. Juan's best friend, _____, won a scholarship to college.

44 Appositive, verb, or prepositional phrase?

Activity

Indicate whether the underlined phrase is an appositive (A), verb (V), or prepositional (P) phrase by writing the corresponding letter on the line before the sentence.

1. _____ The machinist <u>was elated</u> with his substantial raise.

2. _____ LeBron James, <u>an NBA star</u>, can easily score against most of his opponents.

3. _____ Lupita played well <u>in the second half</u> of the soccer game.

4. _____ The boxer used his most powerful weapon, the left hook, very often <u>during the match</u>.

5. _____ Some of the marchers <u>had been exhausted</u> by the hot sun during the parade.

6. _____ <u>Will</u> you <u>lend</u> me your eraser for next period's class?

7. _____ Abraham Lincoln, <u>a man of many talents</u>, was the sixteenth U.S. president.

8. _____ "Red, <u>the color of my aunt's car</u>, is also my favorite color," Mitch stated.

9. _____ Patsy, <u>a mischief maker</u>, creates havoc for her family members.

10. _____ Warren <u>has</u> never <u>forgotten</u> his sisters' birthdays.

11. _____ These ducks <u>in the photograph</u> are so cute together.

12. _____ Physics <u>has been</u> Jeremy's most challenging class this semester.

13. _____ The crowd cheered <u>throughout the concert</u>.

14. _____ Marty, <u>a World War II veteran</u>, was John's uncle.

15. _____ James Short had kept the prized autograph <u>in a safe place</u>.

45 the participle and participial phrase

◗ A word that looks like a verb, but functions as an adjective, is a ***participle.*** A participle is a type of verbal, a word that is formed from a verb, but functions as another part of speech. Common endings for participles are *-ing* (read*ing*), *-ed* (return*ed*), *-en* (brok*en*), *-d* (sai*d*), *-t* (len*t*), and *-n* (wove*n*).

Each italicized word in these sentences is a participle.

Mom's *puzzling* answer confused us.

These *squandered* opportunities will not come again soon.

This *forgotten* soldier will be honored by the townspeople next weekend.

The *paid* workers were happy with their salaries.

Steve's *unsent* messages were still stored in his computer.

A *driven* athlete will push herself to the limit.

◗ A ***participial phrase*** consists of the participle, its modifiers, and other words needed to complete the idea begun by the participle. This type of phrase generally follows immediately after or right before the noun it describes.

The participial phrase is underlined in each sentence.

Leaving the press conference, the politician felt confident about her answers.

A memo sent to all the employees was well received.

The teacher's best lesson delivered to his eighth graders dealt with literary allusions.

My dad's present, bought by his sisters, was a gold watch.

Acclaimed by many critics as the year's best movie, *The Sound of Music* won many awards.

The Sound of Music, acclaimed by many critics as the year's best movie, won many awards.

46 Participial phrase or not?

Activity Indicate whether the underlined group of words in each sentence is a participial phrase by writing PART on the line before the sentence. If it is not, write NO on the line.

① _____ The tourists <u>were waiting</u> for the leader's directions.

② _____ <u>Startled by the loud noise</u>, the parakeet excitedly flew around the cage.

③ _____ The birds <u>soaring above us</u> were enjoying themselves.

④ _____ <u>Leaving her child at nursery school on the first day of class</u> was not easy for Mrs. Plunkett.

⑤ _____ It was difficult for Perkins <u>to remember his neighbor's telephone number</u>.

⑥ _____ The director <u>speaking to the cast members</u> is Mr. Flores.

⑦ _____ <u>Burning leaves in one's backyard</u> is illegal in our village.

⑧ _____ The screens <u>placed into their windows by Patsy</u> had been repaired by Doug Hayes.

⑨ _____ <u>Reading three newspapers a day</u>, Christine enjoyed herself on Cape Cod that week.

⑩ _____ <u>Frolicking with the dogs</u> was fun for Luke's cat.

⑪ _____ Our goalie <u>was congratulated by all of us</u>.

⑫ _____ The young boy <u>running with his friends</u> is my nephew.

⑬ _____ <u>Guided by her trusty dog</u>, Debbie found her way to the market.

⑭ _____ A book <u>read by many high school students</u> is *To Kill a Mockingbird*.

⑮ _____ The gymnast <u>had struggled</u> with her challenging routine.

47 the gerund and gerund phrase

⊃ A **gerund,** the second type of verbal, ends in *-ing* and functions as a noun. A gerund's uses are many—subject, direct object, subject complement (predicate nominative), appositive, and object of the preposition. If a gerund or the entire gerund phrase is removed from the sentence, the remaining words will not form a complete, logical sentence.

The underlined word in each sentence is a gerund. Its use is within the parentheses that follow the sentence.

Learning is fun for Kate and Moe. (subject)

Marcia loves sewing. (direct object)

A fun time for Rachel is reading. (predicate nominative)

His passion, traveling, inspired him in many ways. (appositive)

Geraldine has a love for traveling. (object of the preposition)

⊃ A **gerund phrase** includes the gerund, its modifiers, and the words that complete the idea begun by the gerund.

In each sentence, the gerund is italicized, and the gerund phrase is underlined.

Shopping for new dresses excites Terry Anne. (subject)

The orchestra members enjoy *rehearsing* for long periods of time. (direct object)

Tommy's passion is *running* long distances. (predicate nominative)

Joanna's love, *running*, kept her very fit. (appositive)

Can you pass the test by *studying* very hard this month? (object of the preposition)

Note: Remember that the same phrase can have several uses.

The man signaling to you is my grandfather. (participial phrase)

Signaling to you was not difficult. (gerund phrase)

The player passing the soccer ball is James. (participial phrase)

Passing the soccer ball was hard for that man. (gerund phrase)

48 Gerund or not?

Activity

Ten of these underlined groups of words are gerund phrases. Place a check-mark on the line next to those ten sentences that contain gerund phrases.

1. _____ The dog groomer was <u>brushing Murphy's hair</u>.

2. _____ <u>Making this work</u> will be fairly easy for Kate.

3. _____ <u>Brushing Murphy's hair</u>, the dog groomer seemed to be enjoying herself.

4. _____ Latoya's sister enjoys <u>watching sci-fi movies</u>.

5. _____ Thomas Edison's passion was <u>experimenting in the lab</u>.

6. _____ <u>Launching his boat this summer</u> was a thrill for Jimmy.

7. _____ My uncle recalled <u>walking two miles to school with his friends each morning</u>.

8. _____ These artists <u>working on the mural</u> will finish soon.

9. _____ Monique's arms were tired from <u>lifting all these heavy weights at the gym</u>.

10. _____ Rex's favorite hobby is <u>collecting stamps</u>.

11. _____ <u>Trying to reach his friends by telephone</u>, Willy looked forward to telling them the good news.

12. _____ Hubie detested <u>making loud noises</u>.

13. _____ James enjoys <u>playing his guitar</u>.

14. _____ <u>Illustrating books</u> was fun for Maureen.

15. _____ After that, the commentator was <u>interviewing the country's new leader</u>.

49 the infinitive and infinitive phrase

⊃ The third type of verbal, in addition to the *participle* and the *gerund*, is the **infinitive.** An infinitive is composed of the word *to* plus a verb. Examples of the infinitive include *to remember, to cuddle, to pacify,* and *to yodel.*

Infinitives can function as nouns, adjectives, and adverbs.

To succeed is Ted's goal. (noun—subject of the sentence)

Franklin's goal was *to succeed.* (noun—predicate nominative)

Melissa wanted *to succeed.* (noun—direct object)

Kelly has the drive *to succeed.* (adjective—Which drive? the drive to succeed)

Kelly will endeavor *to succeed.* (adverb—How will Kelly endeavor? to succeed)

⊃ An **infinitive phrase** is composed of the infinitive, its modifiers (or describers), and all the other words that are needed to complete the idea begun by the infinitive.

To stay up later was the child's wish. (noun—subject)

Lorene desired to be a doctor. (noun—direct object)

My cousin's goal was to make the New York Yankees. (noun—predicate nominative)

Henry's ultimate goal was to make other people happy. (noun—predicate nominative)

The musical to see is *Oklahoma!* (adjective—Which musical? *Oklahoma!*)

The strong lifeguard swam out to save the struggling swimmer. (adverb—Why did the lifeguard swim out? to save the struggling swimmer)

50 the many uses of the infinitive phrase

Activity

Underline the infinitive phrase in each sentence. Then indicate on the line before the sentence if the infinitive phrase is used as a noun (N), adjective (ADJ), or adverb (ADVB).

1. _____ Claudio left early to meet his brother.

2. _____ Haley's dream is to revisit Europe.

3. _____ To collect the entire series of presidential cards is my goal.

4. _____ All the students were excited to display their artwork.

5. _____ Kate's determination to teach well is quite obvious.

6. _____ Patsy likes to listen to Broadway tunes.

7. _____ We walked to the pizza parlor to buy some Italian hero sandwiches.

8. _____ My relatives were the most important people to invite to the ceremony.

9. _____ Eloise did try to call you last night.

10. _____ Sheilah was very excited to participate in the contest.

11. _____ The best way to improve your performance is no secret.

12. _____ Is this the proper way to hold the musical instrument?

13. _____ The finest way to memorize the poem is through practice.

14. _____ Lenka opened the book to find the correct answer.

15. _____ To do all of her illustrations well was Maureen's goal.

51 verbal phrase review

Activity

Underline the verbal phrase in each sentence. Then, in the space before the sentence, indicate if the phrase is a participial (P), gerund (G), or infinitive (I) phrase.

1. ____ The teacher helping the English 11 students is Mr. Pryal.

2. ____ The emcee wanted to introduce the contestants.

3. ____ To learn the Greek alphabet was the young scholar's goal.

4. ____ Participating in the Indy 500 this year was fun for the veteran driver.

5. ____ These primary-grade students enjoy drawing on the board.

6. ____ Skateboarding most of the morning, Jason did not tire easily.

7. ____ This speaker is the one to watch.

8. ____ Knowing how to get back to its nest, the oriole started on his journey.

9. ____ Watching the bathers swim occupied the man's time this morning.

10. ____ A man recognizing his mistakes should correct them.

11. ____ Running after his kite was a chore for the little boy.

12. ____ Talking on the cell phone was a distraction for the motorist.

13. ____ She ran across the crowded city street to catch the taxi.

14. ____ The crossword puzzle contest held in New York City was well attended again last year.

15. ____ One day Marcellino hopes to win his town's art contest.

52 matching the phrases in context

Activity

Match the underlined, numbered phrase in each selection with its name and code found in the box. The same code letters will be used in both selections. Each letter is used only once in each selection. All letters are used in both selections.

A = verb phrase	E = infinitive phrase
B = adjective phrase	F = gerund phrase
C = adverb phrase	G = appositive phrase
D = participial phrase	

(SELECTION ONE)

Driving the golf ball more than two hundred yards (1), Phil wanted to do the same on the next hole (2) in this tournament (3). He had played (4) well last week here at Green Valley Golf Course, but he wanted today to be special (5). Putting the ball accurately on these greens (6), a difficult task (7), would take great skill.

1._____   2. _____   3. _____   4. _____   5._____   6. _____   7. _____

(SELECTION TWO)

Have you ever wanted to visit Ireland (1), the home of many talented writers (2)? Going to a foreign country (3) can be a wonderful opportunity. Many people traveling in tour groups (4) like that the trip has already been planned (5) for them. Others choose to tour by themselves (6). No matter how you go, visiting Ireland is the experience of a lifetime (7).

1._____   2. _____   3. _____   4. _____   5._____   6. _____   7. _____

53 showing what you know about phrases

Here is a quick activity that allows you to display your skills with phrases. Do your best!

Activity

Match the items in Column A with those in Column B. Use each number and letter only once.

Column A

1. _____ verb phrase

2. _____ adjective phrase

3. _____ adverb phrase

4. _____ appositive

5. _____ participial

6. _____ infinitive

7. _____ gerund

Column B

A. a noun or pronoun that is placed beside another noun or pronoun to identify or describe it

B. a verb form that ends in *-ing* and functions as a noun

C. a prepositional phrase that modifies a noun or a pronoun

D. includes at least one main verb and one or more helping verbs

E. a verb form that functions as an adjective

F. a verb form that can be used as a noun, an adjective, or an adverb

G. a prepositional phrase that modifies a verb, an adjective, or an adverb

54 happy in ten different ways

Activity

Here are ten tasks to check on your knowledge of various grammar topics that you have covered in class thus far. Every sentence will include the word *happy*! Write your sentences on a separate sheet of paper.

1. Use *happy* within a prepositional phrase.

2. Use *happy* as an adjective that describes the sentence's subject.

3. Use *happy* as part of a gerund phrase.

4. Use *happy* within a participial phrase.

5. Use *happy* within an infinitive phrase.

6. Use *happy* as part of an appositive phrase.

7. Use *happy* as a predicate adjective.

8. Use *happy* as the subject of a sentence.

9. Use *happy* as part of an adjective phrase.

10. Use *happy* within an adverb phrase.

55 writing with variety

Activity

Here is your chance to show how you can use many different types of word and sentence constructions in your writing. Underline each phrase or clause that you use in each sentence. Write your answers on a separate sheet of paper.

1. Write a sentence that contains an adjective phrase.

2. Write a sentence that contains an adverb phrase.

3. Write a sentence that starts with a participial phrase.

4. Write a sentence that ends with an infinitive phrase.

5. Write a sentence that starts with a gerund phrase.

6. Write a sentence that includes an appositive phrase.

7. Write a sentence that includes an adjective clause.

8. Start a sentence with an adverb clause.

9. End a sentence with a noun clause.

10. Write a sentence that contains two adverb phrases.

56 phrases finale

Activity

Write *True* or *False* on the line before each statement.

① _____ A prepositional phrase can function as an adjective or an adverb.

② _____ "Because of" is not a preposition.

③ _____ A gerund phrase can function as a noun.

④ _____ The noun or pronoun that generally ends a prepositional phrase is called the object of the preposition.

⑤ _____ A gerund phrase can be removed from the sentence, and the sentence will still make sense.

⑥ _____ "Called out at third base" is an example of a gerund phrase.

⑦ _____ "We went to the dance" includes a prepositional phrase that functions as an adjective.

⑧ _____ There are three types of verbals—the participle, the gerund, and the infinitive.

⑨ _____ "The candidate to choose is Juan Ramos" includes a participial phrase.

⑩ _____ An adjective phrase can include a verb.

⑪ _____ A prepositional phrase acting as an adjective generally follows right after the word it modifies.

⑫ _____ "To see the beauty of nature" is an example of an infinitive phrase.

⑬ _____ In the sentence, "Removing the furniture from the upstairs rooms was not easy," the phrase "Removing the furniture from the upstairs rooms" is a participial phrase.

⑭ _____ A pronoun can be the object of the preposition.

⑮ _____ The phrase "of the majority" is a prepositional phrase.

57 introducing clauses

A *clause* is a group of words that has both a subject and a verb. Any simple sentence is a clause. Unlike phrases, clauses include both a subject and a verb.

The specific types of clauses are the following:

⊃ A *main or independent clause* is a group of words that can stand alone. "Jeremiah was a bullfrog" is such a clause.

⊃ A *subordinate or dependent clause* is a group of words that cannot stand alone. This clause needs to be accompanied by a main or independent clause to make sense. In the sentence, "Moe went to the department store after she finished her drawings," the subordinate or dependent clause is *after she finished her drawings*, and the main or independent clause is *Moe went to the department store.*

The three types of subordinate or dependent clauses are these:

⊃ The *adverb clause* is a group of words that functions as an adverb. In the sentence, "While Nick was riding his bike, he saw his friends walking along the street," the adverb clause is *While Nick was riding his bike.*

⊃ The *adjective clause* is a group of words that functions as an adjective. In the sentence, "Doris is the woman who designed the mural," the adjective clause *who designed the mural* describes the woman.

⊃ The *noun clause* is a group of words that functions as a noun. In the sentence, "This is what the doctor recommended to me," the noun clause is *what the doctor recommended to me*. The clause functions as a predicate nominative.

58 the adverb clause

An *adverb clause* functions as an adverb. This clause answers any of these questions—*How? When? Where? Why? How much? How often?* It has a subject and a verb, but it cannot stand alone as a complete thought. It needs to be joined with an independent or main clause to make sense. An adverb clause starts with any of the following subordinating conjunctions:

after	although	as
as if	as long as	as soon as
as though	because	before
if	in order that	once
provided that	since	so that
than	though	unless
until	when	whenever
where	wherever	while

Each adverb clause is underlined in the following sentences:

After the captain docked the large ship, her crew members cheered.
  (*When?*)

Because his arm was aching, Mr. Hopkins went to the doctor. (*Why?*)

You can go with us if you would like to do so. (*How?*)

Monica is more intelligent than she thinks she is. (*How much?*)

Activity

Underline the adverb clause in each sentence.

1. While Rome burned, Nero fiddled.
2. Until the weather conditions improve, the boat will not leave the pier.
3. Hector entered the room before we did.
4. Even though Marcelle was tired, she still completed her workout.
5. You can enter the building if you have the custodian's permission.

59 nailing down the adverb clause

Activity

Ten of these sentences contain adverb clauses. The other five do not. Place a checkmark on the line next to those sentences that contain an adverb clause.

1. _____ Do you know when the movie will finish?
2. _____ Because I am tired, I will not participate.
3. _____ Emma left the game before me.
4. _____ Fiona stayed here while we went fishing.
5. _____ Unless I am incorrect, this is their house.
6. _____ Some of the antelopes that were here have been relocated.
7. _____ Larry looked as if he had seen a ghost.
8. _____ Before the band played, we left to get a snack.
9. _____ Did they see where Terry went?
10. _____ Have you seen the principal since then?
11. _____ Though the officer stopped them, she did not ticket them.
12. _____ My brother seemed so tall at that time.
13. _____ Even though you are younger than they are, you are more talented.
14. _____ Because the exam is tomorrow, I must study tonight.
15. _____ After the contest, we will go for a nice meal.

60 the adjective clause

An **_adjective clause_** (a group of words with at least one subject and one verb) is a subordinate or dependent clause that functions as an adjective. This type of clause answers the question, _Which one?_ Relative pronouns, such as _who, whom, which,_ and _that,_ begin adjective clauses. At times, words such as _where_ or _when_ can also begin adjective clauses. If you delete the adjective clause from a sentence, you will still have a full (though less informative) sentence.

In the following sentences, the adjective clause is underlined. Notice the word that begins the clause.

> This extremely intelligent geologist, who is also a talented juggler, has been asked to visit the State Assembly later this month.

> The street that you live on is scheduled to be repaved next month.

> The movie director, whom you read about last week, will be promoting her new film throughout Europe.

There are essentially two types of adjective clauses—restrictive and unrestrictive clauses.

⊃ A **restrictive (or essential) adjective clause** offers essential information that is necessary to complete the sentence's thought. An example of this is, "The trophy that was presented to you is enormous." Here, the adjective clause _that was presented to you_ restricts the information to just that trophy.

⊃ An **unrestrictive (or nonessential) clause** simply offers more information about the noun it describes. In the sentence, "The trophy, which was made in Canada, was presented to you," the adjective clause _which was made in Canada_ is nonessential to the sentence. It just offers more information about the trophy.

61 recognizing adjective clauses

Activity

Underline the adjective clause in each sentence. Then circle the relative pronoun. Finally, draw a line from the relative pronoun to the word (or words) that the clause modifies.

1. Will this be the only instrument that you will play tonight?

2. This next batter, who has sixteen home runs, is only twenty years old.

3. The motorcycle that your dad purchased should be cleaned often.

4. Our former college president for whom this award has been named will be in attendance this evening.

5. Have the answers that you submitted been reviewed yet?

6. Miguel, who won last year's contest, is seeded first in this year's competition.

7. This is the exact spot where the hide-and-seek game began last night.

8. Some films, which I have not watched, were made in black and white.

9. This is the hour when most people should be getting ready for bed.

10. A few graduates whom I have already contacted will help with the reunion.

11. Doctor Gavigan, who is a very competent podiatrist, practices in New England.

12. These proposals that the committee has questioned will be discussed again at next month's meeting.

13. A word that has an interesting origin is *curfew*.

14. Those who chose to leave the session can get the information next time.

15. The only person to whom I have told this personal information is you.

62 the noun clause

A ***noun clause*** (a group of words that has at least one subject and one verb) is a subordinate or dependent clause that functions, as its name suggests, as a noun.

It can be a subject, direct object, indirect object, object of the preposition, or a predicate nominative. This type of clause often starts with any one of these words—*how, that, what, whatever, when, where, whether, which, whichever, who, whoever, whom, whomever, whose,* and *why.*

The noun clause is underlined in each of these sentences. Its function within the sentence follows in the parentheses.

What you thought about that candidate is correct. (subject)

The paleontologist remembers when he met you at the conference. (direct object)

Will these older folks recall how they were part of a terrific generation? (direct object)

Remind whoever is on your discussion panel that we will meet tomorrow morning in the library. (indirect object)

Give whoever needs that information the correct numbers. (indirect object)

Mr. Bellington reminded us of where we should obtain the necessary papers for our licenses. (object of the preposition)

My children's request is that you wear your silly tie to the birthday party. (predicate nominative)

The lady's wish is that you bring her some pansies and daisies. (predicate nominative)

63 the many uses of the noun clause

Activity

Indicate the function of the underlined noun clause in each sentence. Write the correct letter codes on the line preceding each sentence. Each function is used at least once.

S = subject	IO = indirect object	PN = predicate nominative
DO = direct object	OP = object of the preposition	

① _____ These math teachers taught us <u>whatever we needed to know for the exam</u>.

② _____ The winner will be <u>whichever speller correctly spells the most words</u>.

③ _____ <u>When the next door will open</u> is puzzling to all of us.

④ _____ Give the survey's results to <u>whoever asks for them</u>.

⑤ _____ The family's housekeeper scrubbed <u>whichever floors were dirty</u>.

⑥ _____ I asked <u>whomever I wanted</u> to come to the dance.

⑦ _____ <u>Whatever time you decide to leave</u> is fine with me.

⑧ _____ <u>That these clams cannot be opened more easily</u> frustrates Samantha.

⑨ _____ Winning the raffle prize was <u>what excited him the most</u>.

⑩ _____ Winnie presented <u>whoever had earned fifty tickets</u> with a certificate.

⑪ _____ My younger brother forgot <u>that he needed to pick up the shirt from the cleaners</u>.

⑫ _____ You may travel with <u>whomever you desire</u>.

⑬ _____ Fred is very aware of <u>what you meant</u>.

⑭ _____ <u>What was on the screen</u> was very intriguing.

⑮ _____ Working diligently for many years is <u>why Dr. Hutter is a leader in the field of dentistry</u>.

64 adjective, adverb, and noun clauses

Activity

Circle the correct letter of the underlined clause, and then write that letter on the line before the sentence. Finally, write these ten consecutive letters on the line below the last sentence to spell out an interesting ten-letter word.

① _____ Whenever you need a lift, call me.
   (b) adjective clause **(q)** adverb clause **(j)** noun clause

② _____ Give this ticket to whomever needs to get in here.
   (a) adjective clause **(k)** adverb clause **(u)** noun clause

③ _____ The trampoline that is in your backyard is great fun.
   (e) adjective clause **(p)** adverb clause **(y)** noun clause

④ _____ I will assist you as soon as I can.
   (e) adjective clause **(s)** adverb clause **(c)** noun clause

⑤ _____ Can you read while others are talking around you?
   (h) adjective clause **(t)** adverb clause **(d)** noun clause

⑥ _____ This is the computer that you bought.
   (i) adjective clause **(c)** adverb clause **(w)** noun clause

⑦ _____ Pia decided that she will go to college this semester.
   (a) adjective clause **(i)** adverb clause **(o)** noun clause

⑧ _____ Mr. Jones, who is my mayor, will be here this evening.
   (n) adjective clause **(b)** adverb clause **(m)** noun clause

⑨ _____ These magnificent mountains that we just saw are breathtaking.
   (e) adjective clause **(u)** adverb clause **(n)** noun clause

⑩ _____ I understand what you mean by that.
   (y) adjective clause **(t)** adverb clause **(r)** noun clause

The ten-letter word is _____.

65 identifying phrases and clauses

Activity

Identify the underlined group of words by writing the code letter that is found within the box below. Write the letter on the line before the sentence. Each letter is used at least once.

A = adjective phrase	D = infinitive phrase	G = adverb clause
B = adverb phrase	E = participial phrase	H = adjective clause
C = gerund phrase	F = appositive phrase	I = noun clause

1. ____ <u>Writing so many plays</u> kept Tennessee Williams very busy for many years.

2. ____ That man <u>with the golden retriever</u> is Hank's best friend.

3. ____ <u>Unless I have enough vacation time</u>, I will not be able to share that summer rental with them.

4. ____ This presiding officer knows how <u>to attract good workers</u>.

5. ____ The musician <u>signing autographs in the lobby</u> has been there for a while.

6. ____ Joe Edwards, <u>my boss in the factory</u>, is intelligent.

7. ____ <u>On the next day</u>, all the penguins returned to the site.

8. ____ <u>To reach the North Pole</u> was the explorer's goal.

9. ____ Arnold told Juanita <u>that she would probably get the promotion</u>.

10. ____ These are certainly the times <u>that try men's souls</u>.

11. ____ <u>Touching the finish line before the others</u>, the talented swimmer won the race.

12. ____ The doctor's advice, <u>more rest</u>, should be followed.

13. ____ The lions roared <u>while the cats purred</u>.

14. ____ <u>Running in place</u>, the soldier felt fit.

15. ____ These children <u>on the bus</u> need to sit quietly.

66 Do you know your phrases and clauses?

Activity

Fifteen groups of words are underlined in these sentences. Identify the name of each group with its name from the phrases and clauses listed below. Write the code letter on the blank next to each sentence. Each letter is used at least once.

A. Verb phrase	D. Infinitive phrase	G. Adverb clause
B. Prepositional phrase	E. Appositive phrase	H. Adjective clause
C. Participial phrase	F. Gerund phrase	I. Noun clause

1. _____ Win's birthday is April 23rd, <u>the same day as Shakespeare's birthday</u>.
2. _____ The mural <u>had been painted</u> by the school's eighth graders.
3. _____ <u>Until Lucinda's grades improve</u>, she will not be allowed to participate in school sports.
4. _____ We followed along on the trail <u>that eventually led to the canteen</u>.
5. _____ <u>In the interim</u>, let us continue to work.
6. _____ Philosophy is <u>what Naomi will study in graduate school</u>.
7. _____ <u>Will</u> the egret <u>return</u> to this location?
8. _____ I like to visit my former neighborhood <u>whenever I can</u>.
9. _____ The key can be found <u>in the upper drawer</u>.
10. _____ <u>To collect both old and new stamps</u> was Henry's hobby.
11. _____ Derek wanted <u>to win the World Series again</u>.
12. _____ <u>Cleaning up the garage</u> kept John busy last Saturday.
13. _____ This situation is <u>what the director desired</u>.
14. _____ <u>Walking down the darkened stairway</u>, the policewoman was very careful.
15. _____ <u>Finding so many colorful shells</u> was stimulating for Felicia.

67 putting clauses into action

Combine these ideas in each number as requested within the parentheses. Discuss your answers with your classmates.

1. **(adjective clause)** My sister is tall. My sister is in the fifth grade.

   _____

   _____

2. **(adverb clause)** The bell rang. Three mice ran throughout the maze.

   _____

   _____

3. **(adjective clause)** We visited the restaurant last Tuesday. It is in the Sheldon Park Mall.

   _____

   _____

4. **(noun clause)** Here are two magazines. I would like to buy these two magazines.

   _____

   _____

5. **(adverb clause)** School was canceled on Tuesday morning. There was a big snowstorm on Monday night. The storm dropped ten inches of snow.

   _____

   _____

6. **(adverb clause)** Lucy tells us scary stories. These stories are about ghosts. We get frightened by her stories.

   _____

   _____

7. **(noun clause)** Someone will win the potato sack race. The deputy mayor will give a blue ribbon as the prize.

   _____

   _____

68 what good writers do

Good writers utilize effective sentence starters to interest their readers. You can do the same. By using different starters, you use variety, a trait of strong writing.

Here are seven ways to start your sentences.

① Gerund or gerund phrase

Learning was crucial for the new student. *(gerund)*

Finishing his art project on time brought Andy great relief.
(gerund phrase)

② Participle or participial phrase

Smiling, Mom welcomed her guests into our house. *(participle)*

Jumping from the side of the pool, the young boy was enjoying himself.
(participial phrase)

③ Infinitive or infinitive phrase

To laugh is good for your health. *(infinitive)*

To win the trophy was the boater's goal. *(infinitive phrase)*

④ Prepositional phrase

In the evening, Shirley and her friends play bridge. *(prepositional phrase)*

After an hour the cat felt better. *(prepositional phrase)*

⑤ Adverb

Slowly, the children exited the school bus. *(adverb)*

Intelligently, these scientists debated the heated topic. *(adverb)*

⑥ Adverb clause

Because the weather will be good for surfing, we plan on hitting the beach
tomorrow. *(adverb clause)*

Although the doctor will not be in this evening, her assistant can see you.
(adverb clause)

⑦ Adjective

Awed, the circus attendees watched the trapeze artist in action. *(adjective)*

Bright and curious, the scholarship students performed their experiments.
(two adjectives)

Activity

Match these seven ways to start a sentence found in Column A with the appropriate example of that technique found in Column B. Each answer is used only once. Write the correct letter in the blank in Column A.

Column A

1. _____ Gerund phrase

2. _____ Participial phrase

3. _____ Infinitive phrase

4. _____ Prepositional phrase

5. _____ Adverb clause

6. _____ Adverb

7. _____ Adjective

Column B

A. To skate in challenging competitions was Sasha's goal.

B. Brilliantly, Sasha had attained her life's goal by skating in challenging competitions.

C. Satisfied, Sasha had achieved her life's goal by skating in challenging competitions.

D. For her life's goal, Sasha wanted to skate in challenging competitions.

E. Skating in challenging competitions was Sasha's goal.

F. Skating in challenging competitions, Sasha had brilliantly attained her goal.

G. After Sasha had skated in challenging competitions, she had attained her life's goal.

70 it's all about form

Match these ten sentences in Column A with their content descriptions in Column B. Write the corresponding letter on the line after the number in Column A. Each is used once.

As an example, if the sentence reads, "I left my glove with you," the content description will read "Pronoun subject—past-tense verb—direct object—prepositional phrase."

Column A

1. _____ After the debate concluded, the judges made their decision.

2. _____ To understand the translator was the students' goal.

3. _____ Sitting on the old wooden dock, the elderly fisherman was enjoying his day.

4. _____ These old films will be shown in the community room.

5. _____ Watching the business channel throughout the day is my neighbor's routine.

6. _____ Let more air into the room.

7. _____ The play that Arthur Miller wrote years ago is still popular.

8. _____ They will be very happy.

9. _____ Helene was running at top speed during the race.

10. _____ Isaac slept soundly.

Column B

A. Verb—direct object (modifier)—adverb phrase

B. Pronoun subject—future-tense verb—adverb—adjective

C. Infinitive phrase as subject—verb—predicate nominative

D. Gerund phrase—verb—predicate nominative (with two modifiers)

E. Subject (with two modifiers)—future-tense verb—adverb phrase

F. Subject—adjective clause—verb—adverb—adjective

G. Participial phrase—subject—verb phrase—direct object

H. Adverb clause—subject—past-tense verb—direct object

I. Proper noun subject—verb—consecutive prepositional phrases

J. Proper noun subject—verb—adverb

71 sentences, fragments, and run-on sentences

A **sentence** can be a word (*Stop!*) or a group of words that must contain a subject (doer), a verb (action), and a complete thought.

⊃ In the sentence, "Lorina washed her face," the subject is *Lorina,* the verb is *washed,* and the group of words makes a complete thought.

A **fragment** is a group of words that might lack a subject or a verb and does not make a complete thought.

⊃ "During the trial" is a fragment since there is no subject, verb, or complete thought.

⊃ "Vicki running next to her sister" is another fragment because, though it has a subject, (*Vicki*), and possibly a verb (*running*), the group of words does not make a complete thought. Thus, it is not a sentence.

⊃ The group of words "After these stray dogs were placed in the pound" is also a fragment. It has a subject (*dogs*) and a verb (*were placed*), but there is no complete thought.

A **run-on sentence** is two (or more) sentences incorrectly written as a single sentence.

⊃ "The sofa is comfortable, the chair is too" is an example of a run-on sentence because two complete sentences are incorrectly joined (or spliced) by a comma.

⊃ Sometimes run-on sentences have no punctuation at all! An example of this is, "Princeton University is a fine place of higher learning it is located in New Jersey." Here, there are really two sentences that have been mistakenly joined or spliced into one.

72 What's what? sentences, fragments, and run-on sentences

Five sentences (S), five fragments (F), and five run-on sentences (ROS) are found in these fifteen groups of words. Write the appropriate code letter(s) on the line next to the group of words.

① _____ Have you already visited that famous London museum?

② _____ At the beginning of the movie.

③ _____ Let's open the presents, we want to see what you have been given.

④ _____ Last year we photographed some of the events.

⑤ _____ Again after all of the applause.

⑥ _____ Before they started their photography business.

⑦ _____ Please handle these expensive vases with care.

⑧ _____ The men fixing the heater need more time, they can bill us more if they need to do so.

⑨ _____ During the celebration held at the plaza.

⑩ _____ Bring the empty cartons back from the factory they can be used again.

⑪ _____ While you dial Molly's number, the rest of us can continue to set the table.

⑫ _____ There are too many people in this elevator, who can take another one so this one is not so crowded?

⑬ _____ Several telephone operators tried to assist me finally I gave up.

⑭ _____ Leaving through the back door in the middle of the night last August.

⑮ _____ We would really like to accept your invitation.

73 making sense (and sentences)

Activity

All ten groups of words are either fragments or run-on sentences. On a separate sheet of paper, write a logical, grammatically correct version of those words. You can add or delete words, but keep the main idea intact.

Here is an example: "An unfamiliar car in the driveway." This can be changed to "We noticed an unfamiliar car in the driveway."

1. Mount Rushmore is fabulous it is located in South Dakota

2. Before the storm started

3. If you think that it is a workable plan

4. Oliver is a great friend he never speaks badly about anybody

5. James Short just arrived he is funny

6. Skateboarding is wonderful exercise my friends and I like to go skateboarding

7. While the repairman fixed the dishwasher

8. This author had written for seven consecutive hours she was exhausted

9. Looking into the car's window

10. The entertainer sang many songs we like all of them

74 types of sentences by purpose

Sentences have different purposes. Some make statements. Some ask questions. Others give commands, and still others express strong feelings.

Here are the four types of sentences by purpose:

➲ A ***declarative sentence*** makes a statement or expresses an opinion. Use a period at the end of a declarative sentence.

> Andy Murray has a great will to win.
> The commentator laughed at his own mistake.

➲ An ***interrogative sentence*** asks a question and ends with a question mark.

> Are you using the saw today, Mitch?
> May the other people come along with us?

➲ An ***exclamatory sentence*** expresses strong feeling and ends with an exclamation mark.

> This is just the way to do it!
> That is great news!

➲ An ***imperative sentence*** gives a command (strong emotion) or makes a request (mild emotion). Use an exclamation after the imperative sentence that contains a strong emotion, and a period after one that contains a mild emotion.

> Stop that foolish talk now!
> Please take the empty plate away now, Ira.

 **Activity**   Write an example of each type of sentence on the appropriate line.

Declarative sentence _____

_____

Interrogative sentence _____

_____

Exclamatory sentence _____

_____

Imperative sentence _____

_____

75 "purposeful" sentences

Knowing a sentence's design by purpose is helpful. Each of these sentences is either a declarative (DEC), an interrogative (INT), an exclamatory (EXC), or an imperative (IMP) one. Write the appropriate three-letter combination next to its corresponding type of sentence. Each type of sentence appears five times.

1. _____ Have you read this newspaper article?
2. _____ We are late for the meeting.
3. _____ Stop that right now!
4. _____ Remember to watch your step as you leave the room.
5. _____ Are the packages here yet?
6. _____ Professor Franklin said that the situation would improve.
7. _____ Leave those old plates in the closet.
8. _____ That dessert was awesome!
9. _____ Painting is a relaxing hobby.
10. _____ These are the best seats in the stadium!
11. _____ Are the barbers and the beauticians working late tonight?
12. _____ I can hardly bear to hear more stressful news right now!
13. _____ Is this sweater yours?
14. _____ Tough decisions will be made during the next few weeks.
15. _____ That speeding car just missed hitting the bicyclist!
16. _____ Hand me the wrench please, Reggie.
17. _____ She will probably start up the grill now.
18. _____ These disgusting mice have to be around here!
19. _____ Please carry my valise into the next room, Louis.
20. _____ Will you remember to lock the doors behind you?

76 sentences by design (or construction)

Activity

Sentences are constructed by purpose (declarative, interrogative, exclamatory, and imperative sentences) as well as by design. The four types of sentences by design (or construction) are the *simple*, the *compound*, the *complex*, and the *compound-complex* sentence.

➲ A ***simple sentence*** consists of one independent (or main) clause (group of words).

> My report should be longer.
>
> Joanna and Anna brought their children home.
>
> I cannot easily forget that ceremony.

➲ A ***compound sentence*** consists of two or more independent (or main) clauses that are closely related in meaning.

> The sun broke through the clouds, and the children went outside to play. (*This is a good compound sentence because the clauses are related.*)
>
> The sun broke through the clouds, and the television needs to be replaced. (*This is not a good compound sentence because the clauses are totally unrelated.*)

➲ A ***complex sentence*** has one main (or independent) clause and one (or more) subordinate (or dependent) clauses.

> This is the same method that the doctors used last year. (*The subordinate clause is underlined.*)
>
> If you can help us out, we would be very grateful. (*The subordinate clause is underlined.*)

➲ A ***compound-complex sentence*** has two (or more) main (or independent) clauses and one (or more) subordinate (or dependent) clauses.

> [The public address announcer correctly pronounced the player's difficult name], and [the umpire signaled to the batter] who was standing by the dugout. (*The subordinate clause is underlined, and the two main clauses are in brackets.*)

77 simple and compound sentences

Activity

There are five simple (S) and five compound (C) sentences in these ten sentences. Write the appropriate letter on the line next to the sentence.

1. _____ The exciting performer approached the microphone, and the crowd waited expectantly.

2. _____ This operation will take only two hours.

3. _____ Walter signaled for the waiter, and the waiter walked over to the table.

4. _____ Tom, the repairman, entered the office, and his helper brought in the tools.

5. _____ Scratching his head, the musical conductor looked quite confused.

6. _____ The experienced stuntman is capable of performing many difficult maneuvers.

7. _____ Trey's mother-in-law would also like to go to the dance recital, but she already has an appointment that night.

8. _____ Our team's catcher, Jillian, is very agile, and she is also a dedicated captain and player.

9. _____ Priscilla watched the sunset from her bay window across the serene lake in Massachusetts.

10. _____ Can you believe that story?

78 complex sentences

A **complex sentence** has one main (or independent) clause and one (or more) subordinate (or dependent) clauses.

In each sentence, the main clause is underlined, and the subordinate clause is in italics.

After the storm subsided, we went out to inspect the grounds.

The ticket *that you received in the mail* is the right one.

You will be able to ride with us *unless you would rather take the train.*

If the trees shed their leaves during the next two weeks, I could use some help with the raking.

Activity

Part One: Underline the main clause in each sentence.

1. After his assistant arrives, Van will go home.
2. Select a hat that will block the sun well.
3. Rob returned the library book as soon as he found it in his locker.
4. When my pencil broke during the exam, Sheila lent me hers.
5. Isaac gazed at the computer screen while you were reading the schedule.

Part Two: Change these simple sentences into complex sentences by adding at least one subordinate (or dependent) clause.

A. This is the video game.

_____

_____

B. The cars sped by on the highway.

_____

_____

C. Those winds continued to howl.

_____

_____

79 compound-complex sentences

A **compound-complex sentence** has two or more main (or independent) clauses and at least one subordinate (or dependent) clause.

⊃ After the winds ceased, the children went outside to play, and their parents started to rake the leaves.

The main (or independent) clauses are "the children went outside to play" and "their parents started to rake the leaves."

The subordinate (or dependent) clause is "After the winds ceased."

⊃ These maintenance workers who are cleaning up the park after last night's concert are my friends, and they are willing to work overtime to complete the task.

The main (or independent) clauses are "These maintenance workers are my friends" and "they are willing to work overtime to complete the task."

The subordinate (or dependent) clause is "who are cleaning up the park after last night's concert."

Activity Add a clause to each sentence to make it a compound-complex sentence.

① The deck _____
is quite larger, and it will not require much care.

② Several doctors reviewed the patient's charts, and they came to the conclusion _____.

③ Whenever I start to read a novel, I want to get to know the characters, and _____.

④ While the wedding band _____
was warming up, the wedding singer practiced her lines, and

_____.

80 Know the sentence's structure?

Each type of sentence (by design or structure)—the simple (S), the compound (CPD), the complex (CPLX), and the compound-complex (CC)—is used at least once in this activity. On the line before the sentence, write the corresponding letters for each sentence.

1. _____ Several workers placed their lunch orders, and their kind boss drove to pick up the food.

2. _____ Seldom has it rained for this long.

3. _____ Even though Marnie searched hard for the misplaced earring, she was unable to find it.

4. _____ An idea that the director introduced to the group was well received, and then their plans were revised.

5. _____ I would like to visit my cousin soon.

6. _____ The ship's captain made a wide turn, and the boat responded beautifully.

7. _____ Edith sat still while the dentist examined her teeth.

8. _____ Is this the address?

9. _____ When the movie ended, the crowd of people exited quietly.

10. _____ The dealer shuffled the cards, and the players anxiously awaited their hands.

11. _____ A few marathon runners who had trained hard for the event sped along the course, but other less intense runners struggled.

12. _____ These computer monitors that are several years old can be stored here.

13. _____ You can stay, or you can go.

14. _____ She finished her meal in time.

15. _____ Is this the watch that you were given?

81 subject and verb agreement

A sentence's subject must agree in number with its verb. Thus, singular verbs should be used for singular subjects, and plural verbs should be used for plural subjects.

⊃ In each of these sentences, the singular subject is underlined, and the singular verb is italicized.

> Sam *holds* the school record for the mile run.
> This woman *knows* that subject very well.
> Kara *performs* with the local dance company.

⊃ In each of these sentences, the plural subject is underlined, and the plural verb is italicized.

> These two seniors *hold* the record for the mile run.
> These women *know* that subject very well.
> They *perform* with the local dance company.

Activity

Underline the correct verb in each sentence. Then indicate if the verb is singular (S) or plural (P) on the line next to the sentence.

① _____ We (drive, drives) to school each morning.

② _____ Layla (read, reads) her textbook in class.

③ _____ All of the workers (line, lines) up for their checks.

④ _____ Some contestants (win, wins) much money on that show.

⑤ _____ The experienced judge fondly (recall, recalls) her early days on the bench.

⑥ _____ The cereal box (attract, attracts) many shoppers.

⑦ _____ Most writers (do, does) their writing in comfortable locations.

⑧ _____ The replica of the dinosaur (is, are) in the city's museum.

⑨ _____ Today's weather conditions (is, are) favorable for the regatta.

⑩ _____ Seven plane tickets (was, were) given at no cost to the needy family.

82 agreement involving prepositional phrases

A verb will agree in number with the sentence's subject.

⊃ In the sentence, "*One* of the girls *is* counting the tickets," the subject is *one* and the verb is *is*. Both the subject and the verb are singular.

⊃ In the sentence, "*Many* of the girls *are* counting the tickets," the subject, *many*, and the verb, *are*, are plural.

Notice how in these example sentences the subjects and verbs agree in number.

⊃ The *design* for these few buildings *is* intricate. (The *singular* subject, *design*, agrees in number with the *singular* verb, *is*.)

⊃ The *portraits* in the White House *are* memorable. (The *plural* subject, *portraits*, agrees in number with the *plural* verb, *are*.)

Note: When you are working with the indefinite pronouns that can be either singular or plural (*all, any, more, most, none,* and *some*), the verb will agree in number with the object of the preposition in the prepositional phrase that is associated with the verb.

⊃ *Some* of the *newspaper is* missing. (Because *some* can be either singular or plural, match the verb with the object of the preposition. As *newspaper* is singular, use *is* [not *are*] as the verb.)

⊃ *Some* of the *newspapers are* missing. (Because *some* can be either singular or plural, match the verb with the object of the preposition. As *newspapers* is plural, use *are* [not *is*] as the verb.)

83 knowing your prepositional phrases and agreement

Activity

Underline the subject of each sentence, and then circle the verb that agrees in number with it.

1. Many buildings in our city (is, are) managed well.

2. Outside the stores, several men (was, were) chatting.

3. This cryptic drawing, in addition to these others, (seem, seems) to be the work of a very talented artist.

4. The residents of this farm community (select, selects) a new mayor every six years.

5. Both of the monkeys in this large cage (is, are) very active.

6. The persons in this remote location (interest, interests) the scientists.

7. These cans, as well as this bottle, (has, have) been on the ground for several days.

8. A note sent to the senators (was, were) discussed at the private meeting.

9. Particles in the air (annoy, annoys) the flies.

10. Juan's relative from the United States (live, lives) in Denver, Colorado.

11. The antiques in this catalog (has, have) already been appraised.

12. The cartoon monster with the hairy arms (frighten, frightens) my young cousin.

13. Several of the new toys (excite, excites) the children in the store.

14. The pair of earrings (belong, belongs) to my wealthy aunt.

15. These notes on the board (need, needs) to be copied and memorized.

84 pronouns and their antecedents

Take the sentence, "The veterinarian took pride in her work." The pronoun *her* refers back to *veterinarian*, the subject of the sentence. In this context, *veterinarian* is the pronoun's *antecedent*, the word that the pronoun refers back to in the sentence. Usually, the antecedent comes before the pronoun in the sentence. In all cases, the pronoun and its antecedent must agree in number and gender.

In the following sentences, the antecedent is italicized, and the pronoun is underlined.

> The *flag* has lost its colors over these two years. (singular antecedent and pronoun)
>
> Our *teachers* surely know their subjects well. (plural antecedent and pronoun)
>
> *Dogs* know their capabilities. (plural antecedent and pronoun)

 **Activity**   In the following sentences, circle the antecedent, and underline the pronoun.

① This superficial wound should heal itself.

② These girls recalled their passwords.

③ The last time that I spoke with Luca, he said that he would be here on time.

④ When Jim and Joe play their guitars in school, they attract a large crowd.

⑤ Since we called our cousins on the telephone, they have been more friendly towards us.

85 agreement between indefinite pronouns and their antecedents

Singular indefinite pronouns agree in number with their antecedents. These pronouns are *anybody, anyone, anything, each, either, everybody, everyone, everything, neither, nobody, no one, nothing, one, somebody, someone,* and *something*.

➲ *Everyone* in the church is singing *his or her* best. (*His* and *her* are singular pronouns, and *everyone* is the singular antecedent.)

Note: Use *his or her* if you assume that both genders are included, as in the preceding example.

➲ *Everything* in this large closet has lost *its* value over the years. (*Its* is a singular pronoun that agrees in number with *everything,* the singular antecedent.)

Plural indefinite pronouns, including *both, few, many,* and *several,* will serve as plural antecedents.

➲ *Both* of the singers have their fans. (*Both* is the plural antecedent, and *their* is the plural pronoun.)

➲ *Several* of the club officials raised *their* hands with questions. (*Several* is the plural antecedent, and *their* is the plural pronoun.)

Some pronouns can be either singular or plural, depending upon their context within the sentence. These pronouns are *all, any, more, most, none,* and *some*.

In these instances, look to see if the object of the preposition is singular or plural. The verb and antecedent will agree with the object of the preposition.

➲ All of the newspaper is wet, and I cannot read it now. (*Newspaper,* the object of the preposition, is singular; use the singular pronoun, *it*.)

➲ Most of the newspapers have raised their advertising prices. (*Newspapers,* the object of the preposition, is plural; use the plural pronoun, *their*.)

Activity

In each sentence, underline the indefinite pronoun (the antecedent), and circle its corresponding pronoun.

1. Anybody who is here should have (his or her, their) permission slip ready.

2. Because none of the book is scary, you can read (it, them) late at night and not be frightened.

3. Some of these toys have lost (its, their) appeal with these children.

4. The producer said that any of these actresses can memorize (her, their) lines quickly.

5. Neither of those books lends (itself, themselves) to being read in a hurry.

6. Everybody clapped when (his or her, their) favorite dance group appeared.

7. Several of the famous drivers have already finished (his or her, their) practice laps.

8. We heard that one of the performers injured (his or her, their) ankle during rehearsal this morning.

9. Is it true that someone in this classroom has had (his or her, their) speech read over the loudspeaker?

10. All of the sports jackets have new labels on (it, them).

11. Because most of the surgeons had concerns, the hospital administrator listened to (his or her, their) issues.

12. A few of the senators were hurrying to (his or her, their) offices.

13. Any of these radio stations has (its, their) loyal listeners.

14. Many of the seagulls were hungry so (he or she, they) searched for food.

15. Each of the printers has (its, their) own number.

87 indefinite pronouns

The **singular indefinite pronouns** are *anybody, anyone, each, either, everybody, everyone, everything, neither, nobody, no one, nothing, one, somebody, someone,* and *something*. As subjects, these pronouns agree in number with singular verbs.

Everyone in these seats *is* invited to the party.

Neither of the contestants *has* to leave the studio.

Everything in those rooms *was* ready to be moved.

The **plural indefinite pronouns** are *both, few, many,* and *several*. As subjects, these four pronouns agree in number with plural verbs.

Both of the staircases *need* painting.

Many of the brochures *contain* useful information.

Several of the candidates in this year's election *are* debating in the auditorium.

As subjects, **some pronouns** (*all, any, more, most, none,* and *some*) **can be singular or plural** depending on the object of the preposition in the prepositional phrases that follow them.

All of the *pizza was* eaten. (*All* is a singular subject because *pizza*, the object of the preposition, is *singular*. Thus, a singular verb, *was*, is required.)

All of the *pizzas were* eaten. (*All* is a plural subject because *pizzas*, the object of the preposition, is *plural*. Thus, a plural verb, *were*, is required.)

Most of the *project is* completed.

Most of the *projects are* completed.

More of the *room needs* brighter colors.

More of the *rooms need* brighter colors.

None of this *paper is* stained.

None of these *papers are* stained.

88 indefinite pronouns and agreement

Activity

Underline the subject in each sentence, and then circle the correct verb. On the line before each sentence, write S if the subject and verb are singular, or P if the subject and verb are plural.

1. _____ Most of the inspected cars (pass, passes) the examination.

2. _____ None of these dishes (has, have) been washed yet.

3. _____ Everyone in these cabins (is, are) going to the assembly.

4. _____ (Do, Does) both of these tigers eat that much each day?

5. _____ Several of us (want, wants) to be included in the plans.

6. _____ (Has, Have) someone forgotten to sign the register this afternoon?

7. _____ Each of the stockings (was, were) near the fireplace.

8. _____ (Was, Were) all of the pastries delivered on time?

9. _____ More of this speech (is, are) getting better each time you practice it.

10. _____ Nothing on these tables (is, are) mine.

11. _____ A few of the turtles (swim, swims) in the pond back here.

12. _____ (Has, Have) several of these engineers surveyed the grounds?

13. _____ Neither of these essays (was, were) completed on time.

14. _____ Both of these girls (has, have) musical talent.

15. _____ No one on the grade level (read, reads) these kinds of articles.

89 writing with indefinite pronouns

Activity

Now is the time to use indefinite pronouns in your writing. Think carefully about the agreement rules before you compose each sentence. Write your answers on a separate sheet of paper.

1. Use *neither* as the sentence's subject.

2. Use *few* as the sentence's subject.

3. Use *most* as a singular subject.

4. Use *most* as a plural subject.

5. Use *someone* as the sentence's subject.

6. Use *some* as a singular subject.

7. Use *some* as a plural subject.

8. Use *any* as the singular subject of a sentence that asks a question.

9. Use *somebody* as the sentence's subject.

10. Use *all* as a plural subject of a sentence that asks a question.

90 compound subjects (part one)

A **subject** is the doer of the action in a sentence. A **compound subject** has more than one subject.

In each of these sentences, the compound subjects are underlined.

The <u>cat</u> and the <u>mouse</u> ran around the room.

Neither the <u>cat</u> nor the <u>mouse</u> heard him.

Both the <u>youngsters</u> and the <u>adults</u> enjoyed square dancing.

Here are two important rules when working with compound subjects. You will be introduced to several other rules on another page.

⊃ *Rule #1:* Singular subjects joined by *and* usually agree in number with a plural verb.

This <u>plant</u> and a large <u>tree</u> *were* in the photo.

The older <u>boy</u> and his <u>companion</u> *have* the boxes of fruit.

His <u>dad</u> and my <u>brother</u> *are* on the same work crew.

⊃ *Rule #2:* Compound subjects that have a single entity agree in number with a singular verb.

Bacon, lettuce, and tomato is Mitt's tastiest sandwich. (*Bacon, lettuce, and tomato* are a single entity here.)

Chutes and Ladders was Ricky's favorite game. (*Chutes and Ladders* is a game—a single entity.)

All the King's Men by Robert Penn Warren <u>is</u> a good book to read if you are interested in politics. (Though the book's title features a plural noun, *men*, the title is considered a single entity. Thus, the verb *is* should be used.)

91 compound subjects (part two)

Here are some more handy rules about compound subjects to know and use in your writing.

➲ *Rule #3:* When singular subjects are joined by *or* or *nor*, use a singular verb.

> Neither the <u>kangaroo</u> nor the <u>ostrich</u> *was* awake.
> Either the <u>monkey</u> or the <u>giraffe</u> *is* here.

➲ *Rule #4:* Plural subjects joined by *or* or *nor* agree in number with a plural verb.

> The <u>girls</u> or the <u>boys</u> *are* going to the playground.
> Neither the <u>girls</u> nor the <u>boys</u> *are* at the playground.

➲ *Rule #5:* When a singular subject and a plural subject are joined by *or* or *nor*, the verb agrees in number with the subject closer to it.

> Neither the assistants nor the police <u>captain</u> *has* called you.
> Either the police captain or her <u>assistants</u> *have* called you.
> Either he or his three <u>friends</u> *are* going to the library this evening.
> Neither they nor <u>she</u> *is* here.

➲ *Rule #6:* If the compound subjects are in an interrogative sentence, answer the question to see which subject is closer to the verb.

> (Has, Have) either the boy or the girls reached the location?
> *Answer the question:* No, neither the boy nor the girls <u>have</u> reached the location.
> (Was, Were) either the girls or the boy with you at the dance?
> *Answer the question:* No, neither the girls nor the boy <u>was</u> with me at the dance.

92 working with compound subjects

Activity Underline the correct verb in each sentence.

1. *Laverne and Shirley* (was, were) one of my grandmother's favorite shows.

2. Both the eggs and the cream (has, have) been ordered by our food specialist.

3. The bat and the catcher's mask (is, are) in the dugout.

4. Neither the stars nor the sun (was, were) discussed at length.

5. Either she or they (is, are) prepared to address the press corps now.

6. Neither the muscles nor the joint (has, have) yet to be covered in our anatomy class.

7. These cards and that board game (occupies, occupy) my grandfather's afternoons.

8. (Do, Does) the magician or the clowns entertain you more?

9. (Has, Have) these books or that magazine article captured your interest?

10. Either the trombone or the clarinet (is, are) the instrument that you can play in this orchestra.

11. Either the plate or the utensils (is, are) ready to be placed on the table now.

12. *Pride and Prejudice* (is, are) Patsy's favorite book.

13. Both the writers and their publishers (was, were) on attendance.

14. Neither the sailboat nor these kayaks (is, are) on sale until next week.

15. The book's author and illustrator (are, is) Patricia Polacco.

93 subject-verb agreement situations

Here are some important rules and situations regarding subject-verb agreement.

- *Singular* nouns and pronouns use the contraction *doesn't* while *plural* nouns and pronouns use the contraction *don't*.

   This *piece* doesn't look like the one we need. (singular noun subject)
   He doesn't need to exercise that frequently. (singular pronoun subject)
   These *occasions* don't need to be photographed. (plural noun subject)
   They don't remember your saying that. (plural pronoun subject)

   Note: Avoid using contractions in formal writing. Contractions are allowable in dialogue.

- A *collective* noun (a name that refers to a group of people, animals, or things, though they are singular in form) can be used as a singular or plural noun.

- If the collective noun refers to a unit or as a whole, use a singular verb and pronoun.

   The squad is meeting this afternoon. *Its* president is Kanisha. (*Squad* is considered a unit since all of its members will be meeting as a unit. Thus, *Its* [not *Their*] is an appropriate pronoun reference.)

- When a group is considered as individuals, the collective noun is plural.

   The squad brought *their* notebooks. (*Squad* refers to individual members so the pronoun *their* is warranted.)

- Some nouns that look as if they are plural take singular verbs and pronouns. These nouns include *civics, economics, genetics, gymnastics, mathematics, news, physics, social studies,* and others.

   Physics is a challenging subject for Mitch because *it* demands much time and intelligence. (*It* is a pronoun reference to *physics*.)
   Social studies is an interesting subject.

94 more subject-verb agreement situations

An expression of an amount, including fractions, measurements, percentages, and time periods, can be singular or plural depending on its use.

Two-sixths *equals* one-third. (*Two-sixths* is considered a single unit.)

Sixteen hours *is* a very long time to wait. (*Sixteen hours* is a unit of time, one block of time according to the sentence.)

Five dollars *were* left on the table. (These are five separate dollars; use the plural verb, *were*.)

Two-thirds of the drummers are practicing. (*Drummers* is plural; use the plural verb, *are*.)

A verb that precedes the sentence's subject agrees with the subject in number.

In the following sentences, the verb is in italics, and the subject is underlined.

Here *is* a fortune <u>cookie</u> for you. (singular subject and verb)

There *are* seven board <u>games</u> over there. (plural subject and verb)

The title of a book, city, country, film, magazine, organization, painting, sculpture, or song that is plural still takes a singular verb.

(The italicized subjects and the underlined verbs below are singular.)

Des Moines <u>is</u> Iowa's capital city.

The Rolling Stones <u>was</u> my uncle's favorite rock group.

When a relative pronoun, such as *that, which,* or *who,* starts an adjective clause, the clause's verb agrees in number with the noun or pronoun to which the relative pronoun refers.

The woman who is directing the chorus is Ms. Linden. (*Who* refers to the singular noun, *woman*.)

The ladies who are singing together are Kate and Moe. (*Who* takes a plural verb, *are,* because it refers back to *ladies,* a plural noun.)

95 making the wrong right

Activity Each of these fifteen sentences includes an incorrect subject-verb agreement. Without changing the subject, make the necessary verb change.

1. One of my friends are here in this room with the rest of us.

2. The pillow are too hard on my neck.

3. These oranges from Florida is juicy.

4. A few of the painters at that table has finished their work.

5. Before she started her workout, Lupita were listening to the broadcast.

6. The university officials is now admitting more students.

7. Proponents favors this new methodology of training doctors how to be more receptive to their patients' concerns.

8. Then the physician insert the fluid into the other vial.

9. The film festival that was held in the mountains were well attended.

10. Concert attendees admires that singer who really knows how to entertain her audience members.

11. The number of graduates are higher this year.

12. The people in our neighborhood in Queens is very friendly.

13. You does not have to be at the gate that early.

14. Some soldiers is on our train heading for Portland, Oregon.

15. They does not have the winning ticket in last night's lottery.

96 knowing your subject-verb agreement

Activity Underline the correct verb in each sentence.

1. These cards that (is, are) missing from the deck should be around here someplace.
2. Each star on these maps (indicate, indicates) a newborn's home.
3. Melinda's new jeans (is, are) quite comfortable.
4. *Tuesdays with Morrie* (make, makes) me think, cry, and appreciate life.
5. The club's officers (meet, meets) today at noon in the café.
6. The cat that (has, have) been adopted is very playful.
7. The group (leave, leaves) for each game as a unified team.
8. The group members (leave, leaves) in separate cars.
9. Ken's family (exchange, exchanges) gifts with one another each holiday season.
10. Forensics (capture, captures) my interest.
11. Maureen, along with her three friends, (attend, attends) concerts.
12. The Fifties (is, are) the decade that some refer to as "Happy Days."
13. Tonight's news (is, are) not that exciting.
14. (Is, Are) the scissors near you, Antonio?
15. The exercises which (has, have) been recommended to you will increase your stamina.
16. Friends who (help, helps) you are good friends indeed.
17. My new pants (need, needs) to be altered.
18. This is the Web site that (provide, provides) much useful information.
19. All who (attend, attends) this meeting will receive a free ticket to the movie.
20. Robotics (is, are) a topic that James will soon study.

97 subject-verb agreement parade

Activity

How well do you know your subject-verb agreement rules? Here are twenty sentences that will test your knowledge of these rules. Underline the correct verb in each sentence.

1. One-tenth of the test papers (has, have) been collected.
2. Mathematics (is, are) Harold's most challenging subjects.
3. Where (is, are) your books, Princess?
4. They (doesn't, don't) recall that incident.
5. Carrots (is, are) a good source of nutrition.
6. Only one-fourth of your time in the library (was, were) spent productively.
7. One-third of the participants (has, have) their cards.
8. There (is, are) only one dollar left in the box.
9. Where (is, are) your backpack, Carlos?
10. Lyle (doesn't, don't) want to order the food just yet.
11. Fifteen dollars (was, were) my change from the purchase.
12. Twelve days (is, are) left for you to register for the new semester.
13. All of the senators at today's session (wasn't, weren't) happy with what happened.
14. Three dimes (is, are) at the bottom of the pool.
15. Twenty percent of the order (has, have) been delivered.
16. His statistics (is, are) fabulous.
17. Statistics (is, are) my first-period class.
18. Here (is, are) some advice for you, Ty.
19. There (is, are) at least three reasons why you should join the organization.
20. Three-fourths of the process (has, have) been completed.

98 practicing agreement

Activity   Practice using correct agreement by writing sentences that satisfy these directions. Write your answers on a separate sheet of paper.

1. Write a sentence using *and* to join a singular and a plural pronoun.

2. Write a sentence that starts with "Most of the animals..."

3. Write a sentence in which the plural pronoun *them* refers back to the subject.

4. Write a sentence using *Anybody* as the sentence's subject.

5. Write a sentence using *Physics* as the sentence's subject.

6. Write a sentence using the pair of correlative conjunctions, *both* and *and*.

7. Write a sentence using a male pronoun that refers back to the subject.

8. Write a sentence starting with "My favorite team..."

9. Write a sentence using *Here* as the sentence's first word.

10. Write a sentence using a single subject joined with a plural subject by the coordinating conjunction *or*.

99 How well do you know agreement?

 **Activity** Test your knowledge of agreement by underlining the correct choice in each sentence.

1. Mathematics (is, are) Allyson's easiest class.

2. Each of the female contestants took (her, their) place on stage.

3. Everybody, including the pilots in the other section of the plane, (was, were) eager to hear the news.

4. Neither the president nor her closest confidantes (is, are) prepared to address this situation immediately.

5. Most of the photographs have no dark spots on (it, them).

6. These lifeguards (doesn't, don't) become distracted when they are on duty.

7. Anyone who purchased a defective radio should bring (his or her, their) receipt and radio back to the store.

8. Here (is, are) the directions on how to make the dinner.

9. One-fifth of the new physicians (is, are) from other countries.

10. Both of these walls (need, needs) to be repainted.

11. His favorite sandwich (is, are) bacon, lettuce, and tomato.

12. Our captain and team leader (is, are) Emma.

13. All of this carpet (has, have) been intricately woven.

14. Fifteen percent of the quarter's grade (is, are) class participation.

15. *The Outsiders* (was, were) the last book that Rachel read this year.

100 regular verb tenses

Most regular verbs form their past tense by adding *-ed* to the present-tense form of the verb. Examples of this include *walked*, *talked*, and *recalled*. If a regular verb ends in "e," as in *bathe* or *wave*, simply add "d" to form the past tense.

In addition to the **present** (expresses action that is occurring now) tense, as in, "We remember that story," and the **past** (expresses action that has already happened) tense, as in, "We remembered that story," there are other verb tenses that you should know. Following are definitions and some examples of these additional verb tenses:

Present Perfect: expresses action that was completed at some other time, or action that started in the past and continues now. Add *has* or *have* to the past participle form of the verb to make the present perfect.

I have climbed that small mountain every weekend since last April.

Past Perfect: expresses action that happened before another past action. Add *had* to the past participle form of the verb.

We had walked up that hill before they did.

Future: expresses action that will happen in the future.

I will walk with you on Tuesday.

Future Perfect: expresses action that will be completed by a given time in the future. Add *shall have* or *will have* to the past participle.

I will have walked to school by then.

101 selecting the correct verb tense

Activity Underline the correct verb in each sentence.

1. The commercial was (air, aired) five times last night.
2. Have the forensics students (review, had reviewed, reviewed) the evidence?
3. Each of the carpenters has (help, helped, have helped) with this project.
4. Were these models (suppose, supposed, had supposed) to be here this early?
5. Many of these windows (needed, has needed, needs) a thorough washing.
6. The chef (slice, sliced, have sliced) the roast beef.
7. We were (imagine, imagining, imagined) what you were doing at that same time.
8. Some of the newspapers (has been moved, have been moved) to the recycling bin.
9. Will our brother (invite, invited, shall invite) Mona to next month's prom?
10. Hector and the other members of his rock band (had sanged, sang, had sang) at that venue last August.
11. Have most of the light bulbs (replaced, been replaced, were replaced) during this past school year?
12. The ducks that are in the pond behind my teacher's house were (quacking, quacked, quack) quite loudly.
13. Our insurance representative (has been reviewing, review, reviews) our policy for several hours.
14. I (had fall, had fallen, will have fallen) on that slippery floor two days ago.
15. Carlotta (has been painting, have painted, will have painted) portraits for several years now.

102 irregular verbs (part one)

Regular verbs form their past and past participle forms by adding *-d* or *-ed* to the verb's present tense. Thus, *use* becomes *used*, and *call* becomes *called*. *Irregular verbs* form their past and past participle forms differently. The present tense *break* becomes *broke* in its past-tense form and *broken* in its past participle form. The present tense verb *buy* becomes *bought* in its past and past participle forms.

Infinitive	Present Participle	Past	Past Participle
(to + verb)	*(the -ing form)*	*(Yesterday I ...)*	*(I had ... She has... You have ...)*
begin	beginning	began	begun
blow	blowing	blew	blown
break	breaking	broke	broken
bring	bringing	brought	brought
burst	bursting	burst	burst
buy	buying	bought	bought
catch	catching	caught	caught
choose	choosing	chose	chosen
come	coming	came	come
cost	costing	cost	cost
do	doing	did	done
draw	drawing	drew	drawn
drink	drinking	drank	drunk
drive	driving	drove	driven
eat	eating	ate	eaten
fall	falling	fell	fallen
feel	feeling	felt	felt
find	finding	found	found
freeze	freezing	froze	frozen
get	getting	got	got (or gotten)
give	giving	gave	given
go	going	went	gone
grow	growing	grew	grown
hold	holding	held	held
keep	keeping	kept	kept
know	knowing	knew	known
lay (to place)	laying	laid	laid
lead	leading	led	led
leave	leaving	left	left

103 working with irregular verbs from part one

Activity

Underline the correct form of the irregular verbs that appear in *Irregular Verbs (Part One)*.

1. All of the most talented golfers (came, come) to the big tournament last year.

2. Emma has (draw, drew, drawn) a caricature of her uncle spending a dollar that weekend.

3. Did this set of glasses (cost, costed) much money?

4. Has James already (drink, drank, drunk) the entire bottle of water?

5. Ellie (held, holded) her breath as her brother attempted to start his car.

6. These religious leaders (feeled, felt) the need to discuss the event with their congregation members.

7. Three days ago the Umpies (goed, went) to visit the Shorties.

8. Jimmy Baldino (grow, grew, grown) tomatoes in his backyard last summer.

9. You could have (get, got, gotten) better advice about the problem from Uncle John.

10. Have Moe and Kate (chose, choose, chosen) their favorite tunes for the drive to the Cape?

11. It had just (begin, began, begun) to rain when the horses were leaving the barn.

12. Patsy (find, finded, found) an interesting way to repair this float.

13. Jack (fall, fell, fallen) asleep listening to his oldies.

14. Now I (begin, begun) to see exactly how she solved the mystery.

15. Murphy (bring, brang, brung, brought) the scrap of food to his cage.

104 irregular verbs (part two)

Regular verbs form their past and past participle forms by adding *-d* or *-ed* to the verb's present tense. Thus, *like* becomes *liked,* and *walk* becomes *walked.* **Irregular verbs** form their past and past participle forms differently. The present tense *rise* becomes *rose* in its past-tense form and *risen* in its past participle form. The present tense verb *sit* becomes *sat* in both its past and past participle forms.

Infinitive	Present Participle	Past	Past Participle
(to + verb)	*(the -ing form)*	*(Yesterday I …)*	*(I had … She has… You have …)*
lie (to rest, to recline)	lying	lay	lain
lose	losing	lost	lost
make	making	made	made
ride	riding	rode	ridden
ring	ringing	rang	rung
rise	rising	rose	risen
run	running	ran	run
say	saying	said	said
see	seeing	saw	seen
sell	selling	sold	sold
send	sending	sent	sent
set	setting	set	set
shrink	shrinking	shrank	shrunk
sing	singing	sang	sung
sink	sinking	sank	sunk
sit	sitting	sat	sat
speak	speaking	spoke	spoken
steal	stealing	stole	stolen
swim	swimming	swam	swum
take	taking	took	taken
teach	teaching	taught	taught
throw	throwing	threw	thrown
tear (to rip)	tearing	tore	torn
tell	telling	told	told
throw	throwing	threw	thrown
wear	wearing	wore	worn
win	winning	won	won
write	writing	wrote	written

105 working with irregular verbs from part two

 **Activity**

Underline the correct form of the irregular verbs that appear in *Irregular Verbs (Part Two)*.

1. I (wear, wore, worn) these running shoes whenever I go jogging.

2. Cousin Moe (write, wrote, written) a beautiful piece about her second-grade students.

3. Mervin (lose, loosed, lost) weight.

4. Could Ms. Short have (sing, sang, sung) any more beautifully than she did at that ceremony?

5. The court officer (sent, sended) a note about the jury to the judge.

6. Remember that the police officers had already (speak, spoke, spoken) to us about this situation.

7. The small group of musicians had (sat, sit) on this bench during their break.

8. Please (take, taken, took) these plates over to the machine.

9. My shirt (shrank, shrinked, shrunk) in the dryer last night.

10. Jason (telled, told) that joke to us last Monday.

11. Could Kayla have (write, wrote, written) that essay as quickly as she did?

12. The tall boy (swam, swimmed, swum) twenty laps in the pool this morning.

13. This cloth has been (teared, tore, torn) up by the hungry dog.

14. With that amazing catch, the skilled receiver (win, winned, won) the game for her team.

15. Wellington had (ran, run) for that office two years ago.

106 irregular verbs in context

Activity

Use the correct form of each of the irregular verbs within the parentheses. Write your answer in the blank space in the sentence.

1. **(win)** Has this team ever _____ fewer than ten games in a season?

2. **(shrink)** The sweater _____ over the years that I have owned it.

3. **(lead)** This clue _____ the detectives to more important clues in the case.

4. **(draw)** The maid had _____ the shades in the den.

5. **(freeze)** I nearly _____ waiting for the bus to come to my stop this morning.

6. **(catch)** Yesterday, the fisherman _____ three snappers.

7. **(bring)** Have you _____ your camera with you, Mitch?

8. **(begin)** When the game _____, both teams played hard.

9. **(give)** Neither of the presidents _____ much indication of what they had discussed at that important meeting.

10. **(ride)** We all _____ in the van to the mall.

11. **(give)** None of us had been _____ explicit instructions on how to get to the office.

12. **(rise)** The balloon had _____ in no time.

13. **(sink)** The fishing line _____ quickly after I released the reel's lock.

14. **(drive)** My mom had _____ us to this museum many times.

15. **(send)** The misbehaving student was _____ to the principal's office.

107 Correct or incorrect?

**Activity** If the underlined irregular verb is used correctly, do nothing. If the underlined irregular verb is used incorrectly, cross it out and write the correct verb form on the line after the sentence.

1. The police officer <u>catched</u> the thief quite easily. _____

2. My family had <u>eaten</u> at this restaurant several times before last night. _____

3. The truck <u>sunk</u> into the mud in a few seconds. _____

4. The track star could not have <u>ran</u> faster than she did at that meet. _____

5. We lost our way on those dimly lit roads as we <u>drove</u> to Uncle Arnold's cabin. _____

6. Shakespeare had <u>wrote</u> many memorable tragedies. _____

7. A representative from the railroad <u>spoke</u> to the passengers about the proposed plan. _____

8. Neil <u>keeped</u> his cool during these tense moments in the subway. _____

9. Loretta <u>done</u> all her work by herself. _____

10. The powerful dog <u>broke</u> free from her leash and ran quickly down the street. _____

11. I had <u>gave</u> her these peaches for a snack. _____

12. Our candidate had <u>won</u> the election by a landslide that year. _____

13. The proud grandparents had <u>lain</u> awake the night that their grandson was accepted into that prestigious college. _____

14. Wendy and her friends had <u>ridden</u> on that scary roller coaster ride last summer. _____

15. That rock star had <u>sang</u> in many different European cities during her career. _____

110

108 helping out with irregular verbs

Activity

This writer can use your help with irregular verbs (and other writing skills). The student has made many irregular verb errors. Cross out each incorrect irregular verb, and write its correct form above it. For this activity, you do not need to make any other changes.

Last summer, we gone to the Rocky Mountains for our family vacation. On the way there, we sung many songs and keeped a log of our journey. After Dad had drove three hundred miles on that first day, Mom and he decided to stop in a hotel for the afternoon and night. The hotel have an indoor swimming pool. Since last year's bathing suit had not teared or loosed its color, I weared it in the hotel's pool where my brother and I swimmed for a while. Mom brung us some snacks and drinks that we ated and drunked by the pool. I also buyed some ice cream bars that I had saw in the snack shop. Later that evening, after all of us eaten a good dinner, we goed to our rooms to enjoy a good night's sleep.

109 the verb "be"

Forms of the verb *to be* are used very frequently in the English language. It is very useful to know all of the verb's forms. Here is a list to help you along with the verb's tenses.

Present tense: The action either exists or is happening now.

	Singular	**Plural**
First person	I *am* happy.	We *are* there now.
Second person	You *are* tall.	You *are* here with us.
Third person	(He, She, It) *is* in the room.	They *are* laughing.

Past tense: The action was started and completed already.

	Singular	**Plural**
First person	I *was* there last night.	We *were* happy.
Second person	You *were* in the recital.	You *were* excited.
Third person	(He, She, It) *was* there.	They *were* ecstatic.

Future tense: The action will or shall occur later.

	Singular	**Plural**
First person	I *will* (or *shall*) *be* there.	We *will* (or *shall*) *be* there.
Second person	You *will* (or *shall*) *be* selected.	You *will* (or *shall*) *be* here.
Third person	(He, She, It) *will* (or *shall*) *be* on the panel.	They *will* (or *shall*) *be* with us.

Past perfect tense: The action ended before another past action or state of being.

	Singular	**Plural**
First person	I *had* sat in that room.	We *had been* friends.
Second person	You *had swum* in that lake.	You *had helped* my aunt.
Third person	(He, She, It) *had been* there.	They *had sung* with them.

110 busy with the verb "be"

Activity Underline the correct form of the verb "to be."

1. I (has, have) been washing the car for thirty minutes now.

2. (Was, Were) you photographing these beautiful mountains?

3. All of them (is, are) very happy with you, Maria.

4. (Was, Were) they believing your story?

5. My younger sister will (be, been, being) going off to college this fall.

6. The audience members (was, were) awed by the contestant's knowledge.

7. (Was, Were) you and Mickey at the movies on Monday, Monica?

8. I (wasn't, weren't) in favor of these stricter rules.

9. These paleontologists have (been, being) digging intensely.

10. It (wasn't, weren't) a good experience for any of us.

11. He (was, were) blaming me for the problems in the house.

12. Had you (been, being) hoping for an easier trip along the river?

13. You (is, are) the committee's first choice.

14. Many of the birds (is, are) flying toward the tower.

15. (Wasn't, Weren't) you thinking the same thing, Clara?

16. (Are, Is) this the correct address?

17. These magazines (was, were) on the table for hours.

18. (Was, Were) you trying to be funny?

19. (Is, Am) I to believe that tall tale, Tom?

20. You (is, are) going home with the other children.

111 the nominative case

Nouns and pronouns (*I, you, he, she, it, we,* and *they,* to name a few) used in the **nominative case** function as subjects and predicate nominatives in sentences.

Subject examples:

Patsy read the newspaper.

I can assist you with the project.

They will be doing the least favorite part of the job.

Predicate nominative examples:

The new champion is *Tony*.

The new leader is *he*.

Their choices for club leaders are *you* and *Juanita*.

Note: In all cases, an **appositive** is in the same case as the word it refers to in the sentence. Thus, in certain situations, an appositive is in the nominative case.

We neighbors must rely upon one another. (Because *we* refers to the sentence's subject, *neighbors*, *we* is in the nominative case.)

The witnesses are *we* people. (Because *we* refers to the sentence's predicate nominative, *people*, *we* is in the nominative case.)

The proposal's writers, *Jess* and *Tess*, were present. (*Jess* and *Tess* are the *appositives* and are in the nominative case.)

**Activity**

Tell whether the underlined word used in the nominative case is a subject (S), predicate nominative (PN), or appositive (A). Write the corresponding letter(s) on the line before the sentence.

① _____ <u>They</u> will furnish their new apartment soon.

② _____ It was <u>he</u> who found your necklace.

③ _____ <u>She</u> is the first born in her family.

④ _____ The newest employees are <u>we</u>.

⑤ _____ The performers, <u>we</u> pianists, have much practice ahead of us.

114

112 the objective case

Nouns and pronouns (*me, you, her, him, it, them,* and *us,* to name a few) used in the **objective case** function as direct objects, indirect objects, and objects of the preposition.

The ***direct object*** is a noun or pronoun that answers the question "who?" or "what?" after an action verb.

➲ You asked me an interesting *question*. (What did you ask me?—an interesting *question*. Thus, *question* is the direct object.)

➲ The dog drank the *water* and the *lemonade*. (What did the dog drink?— the *water* and the *lemonade*. Thus, *water* and *lemonade* are the compound direct objects.)

The ***indirect object*** is a noun or pronoun that answers the question "for whom?" or "to whom?" after an action verb. If a sentence includes an indirect object, it must also have a direct object.

➲ George brought his *mom* some groceries. (*Mom* is the indirect object, and *groceries* is the direct object.)

➲ We gave *her* and *him* a new car. (The two pronouns, *her* and *him*, answer the question "to whom?" did we give a new car. Therefore, *her* and *him* are the compound indirect objects, and *car* is the direct object.)

The *object of the preposition* is a noun or pronoun that usually ends the phrase begun by the preposition.

➲ Sherry walked into the *cafeteria*. (The prepositional phrase, *into the cafeteria*, includes the object of the preposition, *cafeteria*.)

➲ They sat beside *her* and *me*. (The prepositional phrase, *beside her and me*, includes the compound objects of the preposition, *her* and *me*.)

113 the possessive case

The **possessive case** of a noun or pronoun indicates ownership or possession. Pronouns such as *his, her, its, my, mine, your, yours, their, theirs, our,* and *ours* are all possessive case words.

Here are several rules for the possessive case.

A. Most singular nouns form their possessive by adding an apostrophe and an *s.* (the *baboon's* food; the *girl's* sweater; *Marx's* teachings; *Burns's* poetic lines; *Dickens's* characters)

B. To form the possessive of a singular noun that ends with an *s* sound, take one of two actions.

  1. If a name of two or more syllables ends in an *eez* sound, the possessive is formed without an additional *s.* (*Ulysses'* friends; *Archimedes'* theories)

  2. Add an apostrophe and an *s* if the word would not be difficult to pronounce. (*dress's* cost; *quartz's* essence)

C. Add only an apostrophe to form the possessive of a plural noun that ends in *s.* (the *boys'* gymnasium; the *Murphys'* home)

D. If a plural noun does not end in *s,* add an apostrophe and an *s.* (the *men's* department; the *mice's* hiding spots)

E. Use the possessive form for only the last name in compound nouns for organizations, literary titles, businesses, and relatives. If owned separately, use the possessive for both names.

  Tom's and Pete's reputations (separate reputations)
  Procter and Gamble's sales (combined ownership)
  mother-in-law's magazines (one woman's ownership)
  mothers-in-law's magazines (two or more women's ownership)

F. For acronyms (words formed from the first letters of a series of words), add an apostrophe and an *s.*

  the NHL's (National Hockey League's) members
  AARP's (American Association of Retired People's) membership

114 the possessive case and pronouns

A word used in the **possessive case** shows ownership. Possessive pronouns do not require apostrophes.

The **singular possessive pronouns** are *my, mine, your, yours, his, her, hers,* and *its*.

The **plural possessive pronouns** are *our, ours, your, yours, their,* and *theirs*.

The possessive pronoun *whose* also does not require an apostrophe.

> This house is <u>theirs</u>.
>
> <u>Their</u> car is currently in the shop.
>
> <u>Your</u> notebook and <u>my</u> textbook are in the school's cafeteria.
>
> Is that package <u>theirs</u> or <u>ours</u>?
>
> The movie has lost <u>its</u> appeal with <u>her</u> children.
>
> <u>His</u> bike is locked up next to <u>mine</u> in <u>your</u> space.

Note: Though a noun that precedes a gerund (word that ends in *-ing* and functions as a noun) requires an apostrophe, the pronoun that does the same does not require one.

> <u>Nina's</u> selecting that prize was very interesting. (*Nina's*, a possessive noun/adjective, requires an apostrophe.)
>
> <u>Her</u> selecting that prize was very interesting. (*Her*, a possessive pronoun/adjective, does not require an apostrophe.)

 **Activity**   Fill in each blank with a singular or plural possessive pronoun.

1. _____ diagrams were studied by the medical staff.

2. _____ friends organized a trip.

3. Can you bring _____ photo album to _____ house tonight?

4. Will they not forget to follow _____ directions to get to

   _____ home?

5. These youngsters were happy about _____ choosing Friday for their party date.

115 indefinite pronouns and the possessive case

Indefinite pronouns form the possessive by adding an apostrophe and an "s" after the word.

Is this <u>someone's</u> backpack?

May I ask <u>everyone's</u> help here?

<u>Somebody's</u> cell phone is ringing; please answer it in the other room.

We would like to hear <u>another's</u> opinion.

The <u>other's</u> situation is much different.

If you use the word *else* after *anybody*, *nobody*, or *somebody*, place the apostrophe and the "s" after *else*, not after *anybody*, *nobody*, or *somebody*.

This is somebody *else's* radio, not mine.

Your business is nobody *else's* concern.

Activity Some of the personal pronouns in these sentences require the apostrophe followed by the "s." Others do not. Underline the correct word in each sentence.

1. Will the option be offered to (everybody, everybody's)?

2. (Somebody, Somebody's) car is making weird noises.

3. The pocketbook belongs to (nobody, nobody's) in this room?

4. Remember that this situation is (nobody's else's, nobody else's) matter.

5. We would certainly like to hear (everyone, everyone's, everyones') ideas.

6. (Somebody else, Somebody else's) entered the room after we left.

7. These cards belong to (somebody else, somebody else's).

8. (Anyone else, Anyone's elses, Anyone else's) proposals will certainly be considered.

9. (Nobody, Nobody's, Nobodys') permission slip is missing.

10. (Somebody else, Somebody else's, Somebody's else's) will be assisting you shortly.

116 using the possessive case

On the line provided, write the possessive form for each of these phrases. The first one is done for you.

1. _Lesley's house_   the house that belongs to Lesley
2. _____ the house owned by both Joe and Jim
3. _____ the two houses owned separately by Joe and Jim
4. _____ the car that belongs to that woman
5. _____ the cars that belong to the women
6. _____ the value of a dollar
7. _____ the salaries of the machinists
8. _____ the motorcycle that belongs to my father-in-law
9. _____ the plan of the committee
10. _____ the plans of the committees
11. _____ the suggestion that he made
12. _____ the store owned by Ulysses
13. _____ the address of it
14. _____ the bike owned by Tom
15. _____ the bike owned by Thomas

117 confusing usage words (part one)

1. **accept:** (verb) to receive willingly

   Will you <u>accept</u> this present as a thank-you for your work?

   except: (preposition) but; other than

   All of the dogs <u>except</u> Kenny's dog were in the park that afternoon.

2. **adverse:** (adjective) opposed; unfavorable

   Due to <u>adverse</u> weather conditions, the concert was postponed.

   averse: (adjective) not willing or inclined; reluctant

   Fortunately, the teen was <u>averse</u> to smoking cigarettes, even though her friends told her it was a cool thing to do.

3. **affect:** (verb) to influence

   How will this low test grade <u>affect</u> my quarterly average?

   effect: (noun) result; (verb) to cause to become; to accomplish; to produce

   The <u>effects</u> of the treatment will not be known for several days. (noun)

   This plan will <u>effect</u> immediate change. (verb)

4. **aid:** (verb) to help; to assist; (noun) help; assistance

   The nurse was able to <u>aid</u> the injured athlete on the field.
   Stu came to his aunt's <u>aid</u>.

   aide: (noun) one who helps or assists

   This doctor's <u>aide</u> really knows how to put a patient at ease.

5. **among:** (preposition) used to refer to two or more people, places, things, or ideas

   Sylvia divided the goodies <u>among</u> the five children.

   between: (preposition) used to refer to two people, places, things, or ideas

   Mom divided the chores <u>between</u> my sister and me.

118 confusing usage words (part two)

⑥ **anywhere:** in, at, or to any place

I think that we can drive <u>anywhere</u> in this county.

anywheres: This word does not exist in the English language.

⑦ **as:** (conjunction that starts a subordinate clause); (adverb) to the same degree, equally. (*As* is also a preposition.)

Rex is already <u>as</u> tall as his dad.

like: (preposition) similar to; resembling in some manner. (*Like* is also an adjective, a verb, and an adverb.)

He is much <u>like</u> his brother when it comes to helping others.

⑧ **beside:** (preposition) by or at the side of; alongside

Would you be willing to sit <u>beside</u> my sister and me at the graduation ceremony?

besides: (adverb) in addition; as well

<u>Besides</u> those math problems, what other homework do you have tonight?

⑨ **bring:** (verb) to move something to a place

<u>Bring</u> the boxes back to the table.

take: (verb) to move something away from a place

<u>Take</u> the boxes to that table.

⑩ **borrow:** (verb) to take or receive from another on the provision that it will be returned

May I <u>borrow</u> some money for a few days?

lend: (verb) to let another use or have

Could you please <u>lend</u> me a few dollars for the weekend?

119 confusing usage words (part three)

(11) **can:** (verb) to know how to; to be able to

I think that I <u>can</u> climb that fence with little effort.

may: (verb) to be allowed to

<u>May</u> I help you with those heavy bundles?

(12) **cent:** (noun) one penny; 1/100 of a dollar

Lou found one <u>cent</u> under the couch.

scent: (noun) a smell; odor; (verb) to smell; to perceive with the nose

Do you smell the <u>scent</u> of raccoon? (noun)
I <u>scent</u> a raccoon around here. (verb)

(13) **cite:** (verb) to quote

A respected attorney will often <u>cite</u> several cases in her argument.

site: (noun) piece of land; location

Our favorite restaurant chain plans to build a new establishment on this <u>site</u>.

(14) **continual:** (adjective) happening over and over again

The <u>continual</u> good behavior of the class members earned them free time each Friday.

continuous: (adjective) happening without interruption

The <u>continuous</u> noise of the hammers and saws disturbed the workshop participants.

(15) **doesn't:** (contraction for *does* + *not*) does not

Steven <u>doesn't</u> think that we will need three umbrellas for the beach today.

don't: (contraction for *do* + *not*; considered substandard usage) do not or does not

We <u>don't</u> know what the future will bring.

120 confusing usage words (part four)

(16) ***discover:*** (verb) to be the first to find

The scientist <u>discovered</u> this element years ago.

invent: (verb) to think out and produce

Who will <u>invent</u> a better way to stop people from texting while driving?

(17) ***disinterested:*** (adjective) not biased or prejudiced; showing no favoritism

We all want a <u>disinterested</u> judge to work in our judicial system.

uninterested: (adjective) not interested

Gracie is <u>uninterested</u> in that particular field of mathematics.

(18) ***emigrate from:*** (verb) to leave one country to go live in another

The Greek family <u>emigrated</u> from their homeland and settled in Astoria, New York.

immigrate to: (verb) to come to a new country or area

These Irish brothers <u>immigrated</u> to Manhattan and established themselves there in a short time.

(19) ***explicit:*** fully and clearly expressed or demonstrated

The troop leader gave us <u>explicit</u> directions on what to expect during the trip.

implicit: implied, rather than expressly stated

Our dad's facial expressions <u>implicitly</u> told us that we should not behave in the same manner again.

(20) ***famous:*** (adjective) well known; having fame; renowned

She became a <u>famous</u> singer whose name was known around the world.

notorious: (adjective) well known; publicly discussed; widely, but unfavorably, known

The <u>notorious</u> bank robber had spread fear throughout the city.

121 confusing usage words (part five)

21 **good:** (adjective) effective; efficient; (adverb) well; completely; fully

Evelyn has been a <u>good</u> physician's assistant for many years now. (adjective)
This is about as <u>good</u> as it gets for this group. (adverb)

well: (adverb) in a pleasing or desirable manner; fittingly; to a large extent

I felt <u>well</u> after the challenging mountain climb.
Pierre fit in <u>well</u> with the new group of students in his new school.
These girls are <u>well</u> schooled in how to stay fit.

22 **fewer:** (adjective used to modify plural nouns) a smaller number

<u>Fewer</u> people participated in last year's fundraiser.

less: (adjective used to modify singular nouns) not so much; smaller in size or amount

Edith felt <u>less</u> fear about going on that ride.

23 **have:** (verb) helping verb

I could <u>have</u> finished the recording in two hours.

of: (preposition) used in prepositional phrases, but not in verb phrases

She was a woman <u>of</u> great dignity and service to her country.

24 **imply:** (verb) to suggest indirectly

Did the speaker <u>imply</u> that we should be doing more to preserve the society?

infer: (verb) to draw a conclusion from facts

What did you <u>infer</u> from the speaker's words regarding global warming?

25 **it's:** (contraction of *it* + *is* or *it* + *has*)

<u>It's</u> starting to rain.
<u>It's</u> begun to drizzle.

its: (adjective) the possessive form of *it*

The colorful umbrella has lost some of <u>its</u> color.

124

122 confusing usage words (part six)

㉖ **farther:** (adjective and adverb) used to designate a physical distance

This woman shot the arrow much <u>farther</u> than I did.

further: (adjective and adverb) additional

Let's wait for <u>further</u> instructions before we do anything else.

㉗ **healthful:** (adjective) that which brings about good health; wholesome

Doctor Geiger told his patient to eat a more <u>healthful</u> diet.

healthy: (adjective) having good health; well; sound

If you want to remain <u>healthy</u> into old age, exercise and eat good foods.

㉘ **in:** (preposition, adjective, adverb) within

Sis was <u>in</u> the dentist's chair for thirty minutes.

into: (preposition) from the outside to the inside of

Sis walked <u>into</u> the dentist's office at 2:20 this afternoon.

㉙ **leave:** (verb) to exit; to let be or stay

Most of the children and their parents had to <u>leave</u> once the weather changed.

let: (verb) to allow; to permit

Will you <u>let</u> me take care of your dog while you go on vacation?

㉚ **liable:** (adjective) legally responsible

Because the chipped stoop caused the delivery person to fall, the homeowner was <u>liable</u> for damages.

likely: (adjective and adverb) probable; reasonable to be expected

After we saw that ominous sky, we felt that a storm was <u>likely</u>.

123 confusing usage words (part seven)

(31) ***learn:*** (verb) to acquire knowledge

How did you <u>learn</u> to swim so gracefully?

teach: (verb) to instruct

Will you please <u>teach</u> me the eight parts of speech for this test?

(32) ***personal:*** (adjective) individual or private; intended for use by a single person

This is a <u>personal</u> problem that I would not want to share with others right now.

personnel: (noun and adjective) body of persons employed in an organization or a place

The director said that the case involved a <u>personnel</u> issue involving several experienced workers.

(33) ***poor:*** (noun and adjective) the opposite of rich; not done well

Will you be willing to contribute some money to help the <u>poor</u>? (noun)

Your team showed a <u>poor</u> effort in not running out the grounder in the third inning. (adjective)

pore: (noun) an opening

Harold looked very closely at his skin <u>pores</u> and was amazed.

pour: (verb) to cause to flow

My aunt was nice enough to <u>pour</u> milk into my little sister's cereal.

(34) ***quotation:*** (noun) something that is quoted

The <u>quotations</u> of Mark Twain and Yogi Berra are used quite often for various effects.

quote: (verb) to repeat or cite

Did you <u>quote</u> that author at any time within your term paper?

(35) ***respectfully:*** (adverb) politely

We <u>respectfully</u> acknowledged their country's leader.

respectively: (adverb) in precisely the order given

Please line up these folders from A to Z <u>respectively</u>.

124 confusing usage words (part eight)

(36) right: (noun) claim or title; (adjective) proper; just; correct; (adverb) directly; (verb) to put in proper order

Freedom of speech is one of our <u>rights</u>. (noun)

Is this the <u>right</u> way to tie this knot? (adjective)

Come <u>right</u> home after school. (adverb)

Let's <u>right</u> the wrongs we committed. (verb)

rite: (noun) a ceremony

The religious woman performed the <u>rite</u> in front of twenty people.

wright: (noun) a worker

One of Mike's relatives worked as a <u>wheelwright</u> many years ago.

write: (verb) to record in print

Please <u>write</u> your name on this line.

(37) set: (verb) to put in place

Please <u>set</u> the table for dinner, James.

sit: (verb) to rest in a seated position

<u>Sit</u> down for a while, and catch your breath.

(38) than: (conjunction) word used to compare two or more people, places, things, or ideas

Yvonne is older <u>than</u> I.

then: (adverb) at that time

I <u>then</u> told him that he was doing the right thing.

(39) unless: (subordinating conjunction) in any other case than

<u>Unless</u> you have a good reason, the coach expects you to be here with the rest of us.

without: (preposition) lacking; with none of; (adverb) outside

<u>Without</u> this card, I will not be admitted. (preposition)

He ran <u>without</u>. (adverb)

Activity

Match the fifteen words in Column A with their definitions in Column B. Write the correct letter on the line before the number in Column A. All of these words have been taken from the *Confusing Usage Words* lists that you have studied.

Column A

1. _____ effect
2. _____ discover
3. _____ invent
4. _____ explicit
5. _____ affect
6. _____ fewer
7. _____ beside
8. _____ cent
9. _____ implicit
10. _____ besides
11. _____ less
12. _____ scent
13. _____ borrow
14. _____ imply
15. _____ lend

Column B

A. one penny

B. (used with singular nouns) not so much; smaller in size or amount regarding

C. result; cause to become; to accomplish

D. by or at the side of; alongside

E. a smell; an odor

F. in addition; as well

G. to think out and produce

H. a smaller number

I. to let another use or have

J. implied, rather than expressly stated

K. to take or receive from another with the intent of returning

L. to be the first to find

M. fully and clearly expressed or demonstrated

N. to suggest indirectly

O. to influence

126 Which is the correct word?

Activity Underline the correct word in the parentheses.

1. (Bring, Take) your supplies back to your desk.

2. Will you (borrow, lend) me a few dollars tonight?

3. The Olympic swimmer spent much time training (in, into) the pool.

4. Please (leave, let) me finish what I have to do here.

5. (It's, Its) going to rain tomorrow night.

6. Tell me some of your best (quotations, quotes).

7. Will you please (poor, pore, pour) me some milk?

8. The students were yawning so I figured that they were (disinterested, uninterested) in what was on the screen.

9. What did you (imply, infer) from what the district manager said?

10. A celebrity's (personal, personnel) life should be kept private.

11. Do you have more experience (than, then) the other candidates seeking this position?

12. Are you going to (set, sit) the table for tonight's meal?

13. Do you think that you could (have, of) saved more money over the years?

14. The criminals were quite (famous, notorious) in that part of the country.

15. (Unless, Without) they reach Minneapolis by dark, they might have to go to another motel.

Activity

Part One: Underline the correct word within the parentheses.

1. (Can, May) I have your permission to check the files?

2. As a homeowner, you are (liable, likely) for the damage.

3. Can you throw the ball any (farther, further)?

4. We sat right (beside, besides) the band members at the wedding.

5. My sister is studying to become a nurse's (aid, aide).

6. Wait for (farther, further) instructions about the new plan.

7. Fortunately, (fewer, less) problems plague the police department this year.

8. How many families have (emigrated from, immigrated to) their homeland to other countries?

9. The perfume's (cent, scent) was very pleasant.

10. Should I turn (right, rite, wright, write) here?

11. (Than, Then) I transferred to another college.

12. Will the weather greatly (affect, effect) the bus trip?

13. There seemed to be no parking (anywhere, anywheres).

14. (Learn, Teach) me how to play the guitar.

15. The religious leader plans to perform the (right, rite, wright, write) this afternoon.

Part Two: Write five sentences, each one using one of the words in the parentheses within the above sentences. Write your sentences on a separate sheet of paper.

128 double negatives

In mathematics, a negative number times a negative number yields a positive number.

Similarly, in grammar, when two negative words are used (where only one is needed), the negatives cancel each other out, making the idea positive and not negative as intended. In the sentence, "I cannot get no respect from them," the two negative words, *cannot* and *no*, cancel each other out. Thus, the sentence is really saying, "I can get respect from them," a far different thought from what seems to be the sentence's original intention. Had the sentence read, "I cannot get respect from them," or "I can get no respect from them," the meaning is quite different from that when both negative words are included in the sentence.

Here is another example of this double negative situation. Notice the different meanings when the negative words are included or deleted.

Two negative words in the sentence: We <u>didn't</u> have <u>no</u> disappointments.

One negative word in the sentence: We <u>didn't</u> have disappointments.

One negative word in the sentence: We had <u>no</u> disappointments.

Activity

Correct these double negative problems. Write the improved version on the line provided.

1. Linda can't have no friends over tonight.

   _____

2. The nurse doesn't never give bad health advice.

   _____

3. I hadn't noticed nobody in the room.

   _____

4. This pen doesn't have no ink left in it.

   _____

5. After exchanging their presents, my friends didn't do nothing more to celebrate the occasion.

   _____

129 misplaced and dangling modifiers

Words, phrases, and clauses that describe or modify nouns and pronouns need to be properly placed within the sentence. This placement should clearly indicate which word is being described.

A **misplaced modifier** is a word or group of words intended to describe a noun or pronoun, but is placed incorrectly within the sentence.

> <u>Speaking to the state officials</u>, the microphone held the reporter.

> (In this sentence, the underlined modifier, *Speaking to the state officials*, a participial phrase, is misplaced. The reporter, not the microphone, was speaking to the state officials. Thus, the sentence could read, "The reporter speaking to the state officials held the microphone.")

Other *misplaced modifier* examples include these. See if you can correct each one.

> In the microwave, the man cooked the popcorn.
>
> Unhappy, the match was forfeited by the tennis player.

A **dangling modifier** is a word or group of words intended to describe a noun or pronoun, but, according to the sentence's wording, has nothing to describe.

> <u>To get to the airport</u>, the tram needs to be taken.

> (In this sentence, the underlined modifier, *To get to the airport,* describes nothing. The corrected version should read, "To get to the airport, you need to take the tram." Now the modifier has someone to describe—you!)

Other *dangling modifier* examples include these. See if you can correct each one.

> To solve this challenging puzzling, patience is needed.
>
> Walking along the Thames River, the flowers looked beautiful.

130 revising sentences that have misplaced and dangling modifiers

Activity

Revise each sentence so that the misplaced and dangling modifiers work correctly. Add or delete words as needed. Write your revised sentences on a separate sheet of paper.

1. To move this heavy package, strength is needed.

2. Walking quickly, the road was crossed.

3. Emma read the cartoon laughing loudly.

4. While washing the dishes, my cell phone rang.

5. Glued to the present, Bob saw the bow.

6. Looking under the bed, my birthday gift was spotted.

7. Extending over three hundred miles, the car moved along the highway.

8. Shining in the distance, I saw a star.

9. Wrapped in silver foil, I ate my hamburger.

10. Hal noticed a kangaroo driving his motorcycle.

131 transitive and intransitive verbs

A **transitive verb** is an action verb that has a direct object. Remember that a direct object (a noun or a pronoun) answers the question *Whom?* or *What?* after the action verb. Thus, in the sentence, "The clown threw the toy into the air," the verb, *threw,* is *transitive* because (A) it is an action verb, and (B) there is a direct object, *toy*.

Here are some other examples of transitive verbs. The verb is underlined, and the direct object is italicized.

Danielle <u>wanted</u> *pizza* for lunch.
The old shed really <u>needs</u> *repairs*.
We <u>believed</u> *him*.

An **intransitive verb** is an action verb, but it does not have a direct object following it. In the sentence, "Veronica remained here after the incident," the intransitive verb, *remained*, does not have a direct object after it. No noun or pronoun receives the action of the verb.

Some other examples of intransitive verbs are these.

They <u>laughed</u> quite loudly.
The boys <u>sprinted</u> from the alley.
These scientists <u>know</u> about physics.

Activity

On the line before each, write **T** if the underlined verb is transitive or **I** if it is intransitive.

① ____ We <u>walked</u> slowly around the lake.
② ____ We <u>walked</u> the dog in the park.
③ ____ Reggie <u>wrote</u> your card.
④ ____ Reggie <u>wrote</u>.
⑤ ____ Reggie <u>wrote</u> carefully.

132 Do you know your transitive and intransitive verbs?

Activity

Ten of these sentences include transitive verbs, and ten include intransitive verbs. Write the letter T (for transitive) or I (for intransitive) on the line next to the sentence.

1. ____ These flowers need more sunshine during the next few weeks.
2. ____ Walk more quietly down the hallway.
3. ____ Drivers noticed the many potholes on the roads last spring.
4. ____ Mrs. Littlefield helped Roger find his dog, Rex.
5. ____ You do not need to help yet.
6. ____ A newscaster examined the historical photographs.
7. ____ We witnessed the beautiful sunrise.
8. ____ That hurts him.
9. ____ Bring the tickets with you this evening.
10. ____ My dog ran away last night.
11. ____ The rain came suddenly.
12. ____ Jasmine walked confidently down the street.
13. ____ The heavy winds lifted the table into the air.
14. ____ Larry spoke eloquently at the banquet.
15. ____ Dan rested often during the challenging climb.
16. ____ The scouts marched in size order at the jamboree.
17. ____ Did you give Candace the candy?
18. ____ My dad wished for clearer skies.
19. ____ These candles will glow for a long time.
20. ____ We interviewed Gussy after the memorable performance.

133 active and passive voices

Voice is a verb form that indicates if the sentence's subject performs or receives an action.

There are two types of voice—*active voice* and *passive voice*.

⊃ If the sentence's subject *performs* the action, the sentence is written in the **active voice.** "The pilot landed the plane" is written in the active voice since the subject (pilot) performed the action (landed the plane).

⊃ If the sentence's subject *receives* the action, the sentence is written in the **passive voice.** "The plane was landed by the pilot" is written in the passive voice since the subject (plane) received the pilot's action (landed the plane).

Note: Good writers use the active voice whenever possible. However, if you want to emphasize a specific point, you can use the passive voice. That is why the sentence, "An exciting program was aired by our local television station," is acceptable, even though it is written in the passive voice. The writer wants to emphasize the program, not the television station.

Activity

Indicate, with an **A** for active voice, or a **P** for passive voice, the voice of the verbs in these sentences.

① ___ The construction worker heard the noise.

② ___ The noise was heard by the construction worker.

③ ___ Our contest was won by Timbo.

④ ___ Timbo won our contest.

⑤ ___ A new SUV was purchased by that family down the block.

134 sound-alike words (part one)

The words in these pairs sound alike. Study these quick definitions, and use these words in your writing and speech.

① **board:** piece of wood

  Hillary hammered the pine *board*.

bored: tired of; not interested

  Were you *bored* at the movies?

② **brake:** the stopping device

  Push hard on the *brake* to stop the bike.

break: a rest; to smash or shatter

  The tired workers deserved a *break*.
  Did the player *break* her leg in the collision?

③ **capital:** money; most important

  The company's owners put up the *capital* to start the project.
  Annapolis is the *capital* city of Maryland.

capitol: building

  Each state has its own *capitol* where officials convene.

④ **choose:** to select

  Choose your dessert and take it to that table.

chose: past tense of the verb *choose*

  The couple *chose* their wedding song.

⑤ **desert:** to abandon (di = 'zert); the dry region ('de = zert)

  Did the foe *desert* his army and go to the enemy's side?
  The Sahara *Desert* is huge.

dessert: cake, pie, ice cream, pudding, fruit, and such served as the meal's final course

  We had ice cream for *dessert*.

135 sound-alike words (part two)

Here are some more paired words that sound the same. Review them, and then use them in your writings and speech.

(6) *formally:* in a refined way

He *formally* asked the girl to the banquet.

formerly: in the past

The new soldier had *formerly* lived in Duluth, Minnesota.

(7) *hear:* to use the ears to pick up sounds

Did you *hear* that animal's howl?

here: this place; sentence starter

I placed the card right *here*, and now it is gone.
Here are the finalists in our contest.

(8) *its:* personal pronoun for the neuter-gender words

The contest has grown in *its* importance.

it's: contraction for *it + is*

It's going to be a good beach day tomorrow.

(9) *loose:* opposite of *tight*

The new bathing suit felt too *loose* on the swimmer.

lose: to fail; the opposite of "to find"

The coach did not want to *lose* the game in that manner.

Did you *lose* your keys at the park?

(10) *quiet:* opposite of *loud*

Please be *quiet* in the library.

quite: to a high degree

Winston was *quite* tall for his age.

(11) *peace:* opposite of *war*

Most people prefer *peace* over war.

piece: a portion or part

May I have a *piece* of pepperoni pizza, please?

136 sound-alike words (part three)

Here is the third set of sound-alike words. Study and use them well.

(12) *plain:* not adorned; piece of land

> She wore a *plain* dress to the event.
> The horses moved quickly across the *plain*.

plane: a piece of aircraft

> How heavy is that *plane* with all those passengers aboard it now?

(13) *principal:* the school's leader; the most important

> The committee met in the *principal's* office.
> This highway is the *principal* road in this county.

principle: rule of conduct or main fact

> Jeremiah could readily understand that science *principle*.

(14) *their:* owned by a group

> *Their* clubhouse was made by Frank Miller.

there: place; sentence starter

> He lives right *there*.
> *There* are many reasons to vote for Brianna Feller.

they're: contraction for *they + are*

> *They're* moving to Canada after the school year ends.

(15) *theirs:* possessive of *their*

> That boat is *theirs*.

there's: contraction for *there + is*

> *There's* my dad on his motorcycle.

(16) *to:* preposition; start of an infinitive

> He went *to* school.
> "*To* be" is an infinitive.

too: more than enough

> Perry was *too* tired to run fast.

two: one plus one

> *Two* people were approaching the door.

137 sound-alike words (part four)

Here is the last of the sound-alike words. Study, review, and use them when you can.

17. **threw:** past tense of *to throw*

    The hurler *threw* his best pitch right down the middle of the plate.

    through: preposition meaning "in one side and out the other"

    We walked *through* the many corridors of the large building.

18. **waist:** the middle portion of one's body

    He exercised to decrease the size of his *waist*.

    waste: garbage

    The *waste* paper basket was in the corner.

19. **weak:** opposite of *strong*

    After running twenty-six miles, the runner felt *weak*.

    week: the seven-day unit of time

    Sunday is considered the first day of the *week*.

20. **weather:** outdoor conditions

    Will the *weather* be good for our picnic tomorrow?

    whether: a word used for alternatives

    I did not know *whether* to go to the cafeteria or to stay in the auditorium.

21. **who's:** contraction of *who + is*

    Who's knocking at the door?

    whose: possessive of *who*

    Whose problem is it—yours or mine?

22. **your:** possessive of *you*

    Is this *your* new backpack?

    you're: contraction of *you + are*

    You're the lucky prizewinner.

138 making your mark with sound-alike words

Activity

On the line next to each numbered sentence, write the corresponding letter of the correct word in each sentence. If your answers are correct, you will spell a fifteen-letter word that will help this activity's title make sense.

1. ___ I was not (H) board (F) bored at the concert.
2. ___ They will need to (I) break (A) brake the window to get into the shed.
3. ___ Will you (M) chose (N) choose me to lead the game?
4. ___ What's for (P) desert (G) dessert?
5. ___ Liam was dressed (E) formally (L) formerly for the big event.
6. ___ May I have a (B) peace (R) piece of that cake?
7. ___ (P) It's (E) Its going to be sunny tomorrow.
8. ___ You will need to be more (D) quite (R) quiet because your father is sleeping.
9. ___ Have they introduced the new school (I) principal (H) principle, Ms. Morrison?
10. ___ The (S) plain (N) plane landed two miles away from here.
11. ___ (T) There (S) Their are many good reasons to attend that college.
12. ___ Is that (E) there (I) their fence?
13. ___ I am (O) to (N) too tired to read and understand this passage.
14. ___ My sister will start her new job next (A) weak (G) week.
15. ___ (S) Whose (N) Who's books are on my desk?

The fifteen-letter word is _____.

139 regular comparison of adjectives and adverbs

To show how they differ in degree or extent, most adjectives and adverbs have three degrees (or forms)—the *positive,* the *comparative,* and the *superlative.*

One-syllable words form these degrees in a regular way.

➲ The **positive degree (or form)** is used when an adjective or adverb modifier is *not* being compared. The *young* sister walked with her brother. (*Young* simply states the sister's age.)

➲ The **comparative degree (or form)** is used when two people, places, things, or ideas are compared. Add *-er* to these words to form the comparative. The *younger* sister walked with her father. (The sister's age is being compared to the age of another sister.)

➲ The **superlative degree (or form)** is used when more than two people, places, things, or ideas are compared. Add *-est* to these words to form the superlative. The *youngest* sister walked with her mother. (The sister's age is compared to the ages of at least two other sisters.)

Positive Degree	Comparative Degree	Superlative Degree
tall	taller	tallest
fast	faster	fastest
large	larger	largest
small	smaller	smallest
light	lighter	lightest

Activity

Fill in each blank with the correct form of the word in parentheses.

① **(smart)** Johnny is the _____ of the twenty students.

② **(nice)** Mary is the _____ of the four directors.

③ **(bright)** This new wallpaper is _____.

④ **(smooth)** This board is _____ than the other one.

⑤ **(long)** "This is the _____ song that I have ever heard," stated Julio.

142

140 irregular comparison of adjectives and adverbs

Adjectives and adverbs of two or more syllables form their comparative and superlative degrees (or forms) in an irregular way. The rules below will help you understand and utilize these forms.

⟳ Use -er, more, or less to form the comparative degree of many two-syllable modifiers or describers.

⟳ Adverbs that end in -ly always use more or less to form the comparative degree and most and least to form the superlative degree.

⟳ When forming the comparative and superlative degrees of modifiers (adjectives and adverbs) that have two syllables, "Let your ear be your gear." In other words, if adding -er or -est makes the word hard or clumsy to pronounce, use more (or less) and most (or least) instead.

⟳ Modifiers of three or more syllables, such as *intelligent*, *cumbersome*, and *beautiful*, always form their comparative degrees with *more* (or *less*) and their superlative degrees with *most* (or *least*). Examples include *less magnificent*, *more interesting*, and *most spectacular*.

Positive Degree	Comparative Degree	Superlative Degree
lovely	more lovely	most lovely
funny	funnier	funniest
crowded	less crowded	least crowded
plentiful	more plentiful	most plentiful

Activity   Fill in each blank with the correct form of the word in parentheses.

① **(frightened)** My dog is the _____ of all those dogs in the kennel.

② **(rigorous)** Eddie feels that the rope climb is a _____ exercise than the push-up.

③ **(happy)** Are you _____ today than you were yesterday?

SECTION THREE

Mechanics

141 periods, question marks, and exclamation marks

① Use a **period** at the end of a declarative sentence, a sentence that is a request, and one that includes a mild command.

> Our blue couch will soon be replaced. (declarative sentence)
>
> Please help me. (request)
>
> Let's be quiet. (mild command)

② Use a **period** after abbreviations.

> Dr. (Doctor)   Mr. (Mister)   ft. (foot)   in. (inch)

③ Use a **question mark** at the end of an interrogative sentence.

> Have you finished your dinner, Sven?

Note: The speaker's exact words should be placed within the quotation marks. If those words form a question, place the question mark inside the quotation marks.

> Jason asked, "Is this my slice of pizza?"

Note: If the speaker's exact words are a statement but are within a sentence that asks a question, place the question mark outside the quotation marks.

> Did Mollie say, "Tomorrow is the deadline"?

④ Use an **exclamation mark** at the end of an exclamatory sentence.

> This is too good to be true!

Note: If a speaker's exact words require an exclamation mark, place that mark within the quotation marks.

> "What a great performance!" Emma remarked to James.

Note: If a speaker's exact words are a statement, and the entire sentence is an exclamation, place the exclamation mark outside the quotation marks.

> It is hard to believe that Mark ever said, "I think that you're right"!

146

142 working with periods, question marks, and exclamation marks

 **Activity** Place the appropriate periods, questions marks, and exclamation marks as needed. All other punctuation marks have already been inserted.

1. Can you remember your previous four phone numbers, Kyle

2. "I wish that this test was already over," John Smithers said

3. Sheryl asked, "Have any of those chickens crossed the road yet"

4. Great You can see that these are the winning lottery numbers

5. Should these plants be moved into the shed for the season

6. Jackson exclaimed, "This party is absolutely terrific"

7. Did Anne say, "My coat is in the auditorium"

8. What is that extremely annoying sound

9. Please take that book to the bookmobile, Chauncey

10. Let's see what surprises the workers have in store for us

11. "Was John Lewis with you during the experiment" the professor asked her assistant

12. Tell all of them to get down here immediately—or else

13. Please call the housekeeper when you get a chance

14. The office manager asked his maintenance official, "When will you be able to have your workers wash these windows"

15. "Did William Shakespeare, the renowned playwright, really write all of those plays, or did somebody else write some, or most, or all of them" the English teacher asked her students

143 commas (part one)

A *comma* probably has more rules and uses than any other punctuation mark. Below is an important comma rule.

① Use commas to separate items (words, phrases, and clauses) in a series.

James enjoys playing tennis, soccer, and basketball. (words in a series)

The troop traveled into the mountains, across the plains, and along the river. (phrases in a series)

The car dealer made sure that the purchaser's car was clean, that the license plates were ready, and that the ownership papers had been signed. (clauses in a series)

Note: If all the items in a series are joined by *and, or,* or *nor,* commas are not required.

The chef's exquisite dishes include filet mignon and roast beef and lamb.

Note: If the conjunction *and* joins words that constitute a unit, team, or such, do not separate that name. Yet, you will still need the commas to separate items in a series.

Peanut butter and jelly, ham and eggs, and spaghetti and meatballs are the children's favorite foods.

Note: Some writers choose not to include the final comma in a series if by leaving the comma out, the meaning is still clear.

Our social studies class members studied the Korean War, the Civil War, World War I and World War II. (It is clear that the social studies students studied four wars.)

144 commas (part two)

Here are some useful rules when you are working with commas.

② Use a comma after *Yes* and *No* when these words start a sentence.

> *Yes*, we have the show's starting time.
>
> *No*, there are no bananas in that store.

③ Use a comma both after consecutive introductory prepositional phrases and after a long introductory prepositional phrase.

> *In the middle of New York City,* the traffic is very heavy during rush hour.
>
> *In the World Series' final game that was played in 1960,* the Pirates hitter whacked a home run over the left field wall.

Note: A comma can be placed after a short introductory prepositional phrase if the sentence's meaning and flow are improved by the comma. Read the sentence aloud to see if a comma is justified.

> *In the first instance,* the dog was in the back of the van.
>
> *Without Greg's assistance,* Ricardo would have spent many hours on that project.

④ Use a comma after an introductory participle or participial phrase.

> *Intrigued,* the young child looked into the fishbowl.
>
> *Motivated by their drama coach's remarks,* the cast members worked even harder than before.

⑤ Use a comma after an introductory adverb clause.

> *Before we started our vacation,* we had the mechanic check out our car.

Note: In most instances (unless the sentence's meaning is unclear), an adverb clause that follows an independent clause is not preceded by a comma.

> I cannot recall a single instance *when Jimmy was inconsiderate.*

145 commas (part three)

Here are some additional helpful comma rules.

6 Use a comma to separate two or more adjectives that precede a noun. To check if a comma is needed, separate the two adjectives with the word <u>and</u>. If it sounds logical, a comma is required.

> She is an *intelligent, fair* leader.
>
> The draftee is a *strong, athletic* player.

Note: In the sentence, "We were served fried green tomatoes as part of our meal," *fried* is an adverb, not another adjective. Thus, a comma is not necessary.)

7 Use a comma to separate independent clauses joined by the conjunctions *for, and, nor, but, or,* and *yet.*

> The singer wanted to perform at Carnegie Hall, *but* her schedule prevented that.
>
> You can drive, *or* you can walk.

Note: When you use the conjunctions *for*, *so*, and *yet* to join independent clauses, always use a comma before the conjunction. For the conjunctions *and*, *nor*, *but*, and *or*, a comma is not required as long as the independent clauses are relatively short, AND the sentence is understandable and clear without the comma.

> Our principal understood *and* she responded immediately. (no comma needed)

8 Use a comma to set off a word or words in direct address.

> *Ellie,* would you like us to pull you on the float again?
>
> This situation, *Eve,* is drastic.
>
> Will you lend a hand here, *Nicky*?

9 Use a comma to set off parenthetical (provides additional information and is loosely connected to the sentence's content) expressions, such as, "I believe," "For example," "On the other hand," "In the first place," "As a matter of fact," "To tell the truth," "Of course," and "However."

> This, *I believe,* is the best method.

146 commas (part four)

Here is a very important comma rule. Study it, and use it well in your writing.

⑩ Use a comma to separate nonessential or nonrestrictive clauses, participial phrases, and appositives. A *nonessential* or *nonrestrictive* element adds information that is not necessary to the sentence's basic meaning.

- Nonessential or nonrestrictive clauses

  The debate, *which was attended by two hundred people,* was exciting. (The fact that two hundred people attended the debate is not essential to the sentence's basic meaning.)

  ESSENTIAL CLAUSES: (Each underlined clause restricts the italicized word that it modifies.)

  The *dress* that Mom wore to the dinner last night was a gift from Dad.

  A *man* who has confidence will go far.

- Nonessential or nonrestrictive participial phrases

  My two buddies, *posing for their high school reunion photo,* have worked for the government for the past thirty years. (The fact that these two buddies are posing for their high school reunion photo is not essential to the sentence's meaning.)

  ESSENTIAL PARTICIPIAL PHRASES: (Each underlined phrase restricts the italicized word that it modifies.)

  These *cards* left on the table belong to Gino.

  The *woman* hailing the cab is my sister.

- Nonessential or nonrestrictive appositives

  Stuart, my best friend, loves to laugh.

  ESSENTIAL APPOSITIVE PHRASES: (Each underlined appositive phrase restricts the italicized word that it modifies.)

  Has your music *teacher,* Mrs. Brennan, given you the assignment?

  The *address,* 1313 Mockingbird Lane, should ring a bell with television viewers of that era.

147 commas (part five)

Here are some additional useful rules when working with the comma.

11 Use a comma after the salutation of a friendly letter.

> Dear Marty,
> Dearest Mom,

12 Use a comma after the closing in a friendly or business letter.

> Sincerely,
> Be well,

13 Use a comma to separate items in dates and addresses.

> She was born on January 4, 1993, in Baton Rouge, Louisiana.
> The family's current address is 1600 Pennsylvania Avenue, Washington, DC.

Note: A comma is not needed

- between the month and the day—April 18, 2010
- between the month and the year (when no day is offered)—January 2020
- between the state (or state's abbreviation) and the ZIP Code—Canton, MA 02021
- between the house or apartment number and the street—204 Joyner Court or Apartment 6A Twelfth Street

14 Use a comma to separate the speaker from the speaker's direct quotation.

> Trey remarked, "This blanket was already washed."
> "My car needs new tires," Gabriella said.

Note: Place the period and comma within the closing quotation marks.

15 Use a comma after a mild interjection.

> Oh, I didn't realize that you were here, Nana.

Note: Use an exclamation mark after a strong interjection.

> Rats! I left my wallet at the beach.

148 commas in action

Activity Insert commas where needed. Each sentence needs at least one comma.

1. Wendall would like to go fishing but his father needs his help on the farm.

2. If Julio had not corrected the error he would have earned a lower grade.

3. Because Julianne studied diligently for the examination she passed with flying colors.

4. The long exhausting journey finally ended.

5. My dad met my mom on June 14 1975.

6. Clara asked "Are these your violin strings?"

7. The family members visited New Orleans Detroit Chicago and Los Angeles.

8. "I moved from California to Utah last year" the salesman declared.

9. Dear Nicolina (as the salutation of a friendly letter)

10. Smitty will you please open that door for me?

11. Mr. Pryal the esteemed English teacher knows the lyrics of many old songs.

12. Our friends who are good bowlers will travel to Spain this fall.

13. Since you look younger than twenty-one years old I will need to see some identification.

14. Within a few weeks after her interview the movie actress purchased a home in Hollywood.

15. As a matter of fact this is the way home.

16. Hector married Louanna on August 7 2006.

17. Stunned by the powerful punch the boxer retreated to his corner.

18. Needless to say the Fourth of July celebration was joyous.

19. Sincerely (as the closing of a letter)

20. Yes this is the man I will marry next year.

149 some more commas in action

Insert commas where they are required. Each sentence needs at least one comma.

1. After the initial stage of the project the manager made three changes.
2. Your neighbor who has three dogs in his backyard is the local bank president.
3. Yours truly (as the closing of a letter)
4. Well you can probably get there by then.
5. Excited by the news the cameraman sprinted to the scene.
6. Dearest Dad (the salutation of a friendly letter)
7. Can you read the next paragraph Rachel?
8. "This documentary is very informative" Roger told Ray.
9. To tell the truth my sister already knows about your plan.
10. Because Eddie needs a ride I volunteered to take him.
11. As soon as the song was played the children began to sing and dance.
12. Yes you should begin the game without me.
13. These dogs bark loudly and those cats love to scurry around the house.
14. He lives in Richmond Virginia.
15. Dan Marino who quarterbacked the Miami Dolphins for years was always a threat to pass for a touchdown.
16. Joyce the Little League representative has been volunteering for many seasons.
17. The skilled carpenter purchased nails hammers crowbars and putty at the local hardware store.
18. Sincerely yours (as the closing of a letter)
19. He was my first choice but the committee members thought differently.
20. The meteorologist answered your brilliant intriguing question.

150 comma matching contest

Activity

Match the reasons for using a comma in Column A with their examples in Column B. Each answer is used only once. Write the letter from Column B on the line in Column A. The first one is done for you.

Column A

1. __C__ after the salutation of a friendly letter

2. _____ after the closing of a friendly or business letter

3. _____ to separate items in dates and addresses

4. _____ to separate the speaker from the quotation

5. _____ to set off consecutive introductory prepositional phrases

6. _____ to separate nonessential or nonrestrictive clause

7. _____ to separate two or more adjectives that precede a noun

8. _____ to separate independent clauses joined by a conjunction

9. _____ to set off words in direct address

10. _____ after an introductory participial phrase

Column B

A. In the middle of the night, the crickets were making loud noises.

B. Matthew asked, "Are we meeting here this afternoon?"

C. Dear Samantha,

D. Hunted down by the police, the criminal was finally caught.

E. A considerate, intelligent person will inform you.

F. Sincerely,

G. We shot the toothpaste commercial, but it has not aired yet.

H. Shawneeta, is that you in the picture?

I. I met you on August 30, 2007.

J. These veterans, who are going to the banquet later, all served in the Korean War.

151 the apostrophe

Here are useful rules for the apostrophe. Learn them well, and use them in your writing.

① Use an apostrophe to form the possessive of singular and plural nouns.
Add an apostrophe and an *s* to form the possessive of a singular noun.

> Joe + 's = Joe's car   flag + 's = flag's colors
> day + 's = day's effort   glass + 's = glass's cost

Note: If a plural noun ends in *s,* just add an apostrophe.

> cars + ' = cars' interiors
> televisions + ' = televisions' locations

Note: If a plural noun does not end in *s,* add 's to the word.

> mice + 's = mice's home
> women + 's = women's department

Note: If a name of two or more syllables ends in an *eez* sound, the possessive is formed without an additional *s.*

> the tales of Ulysses = Ulysses' tales
> the speeches of Orestes = Orestes' speeches

② To make the possessive of a compound word or the name of a co-owned business or organization, add 's to the last word of the name.

> brother-in-law's shoes
> Jackson and Meyer's law firm

Activity Make each phrase possessive. Write your answer on the line provided.

A. _____ the pictures owned by Mary

B. _____ the coat owned by the sister-in-law of John

C. _____ the speech delivered by Les

D. _____ the space owned by Fred and Garrett

E. _____ the address of Demetrius

156

152 more apostrophe situations

Here are more situations involving the use of the apostrophe. Review them, and incorporate them into your writing.

① Use an apostrophe in contractions (words that combine two words into one).

had not = hadn't	were not = weren't	you would = you'd
would not = wouldn't	I will = I'll	was not = wasn't

② Form the plural of a lowercase letter by placing an *'s* after the letter.

There are three *a's* in that word.

Mind your *p's* and *q's*.

You *do not* have to add an apostrophe to form the plural of capitalized letters, numbers, or symbols.

We counted three *Ts* in that paragraph. (capitalized letters)

How many *8s (or eights)* are in that column? (numbers)

Earl loves to use *$s (or dollar signs)* in his writing. (symbols)

③ Use an apostrophe to show where the letter(s) is left out in a word or number.

The Class of '18 = The Class of 2018

Let's = Let us

Gregory's = Gregory is or Gregory has

④ Use an apostrophe to form the plural of an abbreviation that ends with a period.

B.A.'s (or BAs) = Bachelors of Arts

M.A.'s (or MAs) = Masters of Arts

PhD.'s (or PhDs) = Doctors of Philosophy

P.A.'s (or PAs) = Physicians Assistants

⑤ Use an apostrophe to form the plural of an abbreviation that is not followed by a period. It is also acceptable to write the plural without the period.

How many *CD's (or CDs)* do you own?

How many different *LSAT's (or LSATs)* has Bertha taken?

153 working with apostrophes

On the line next to each number, form the possessive form of the person, place, or thing using an apostrophe.

1. _____ the scarf that belongs to the woman

2. _____ the scarf that belongs to Helen

3. _____ the scarves that belong to the women

4. _____ the bike that is owned by the boy

5. _____ the bike that is owned by Chris

6. _____ the bikes that are owned by the boys

7. _____ the room occupied by the baby

8. _____ the room occupied by the babies

9. _____ the opinions of everybody

10. _____ the ideas of my uncle

11. _____ the backpack belonging to someone

12. _____ the home of my brother-in-law

13. _____ the car owned by Jim and Nicole

14. _____ the cars separately owned by Nicole and Jim

15. _____ the magazine of this month

154 the colon

1. Use a colon (:) to introduce a list or series of items.

    You should have the following books and supplies with you on the first day of class: *Roget's Thesaurus,* two pencils, a dictionary, and two notebooks.

    These are the eight parts of speech: noun, pronoun, adjective, verb, adverb, preposition, conjunction, and interjection.

    Note: A colon should <u>not</u> follow directly after a verb or a preposition. The following two sentences include *incorrect* uses of the colon.

    The two days of the weekend are: Saturday and Sunday.

    We saw our dog run into: the woods, the house, and the neighbor's backyard.

2. Use a colon after the salutation of a business letter.

    Dear Sirs:

    Dear Madam:

3. Use a colon between the hour and the minute of time.

    It is now 4:22.

    The train is due here at 5:08.

4. Use a colon between a title and a subtitle.

    Mary Shelley wrote the novel *Frankenstein: or, the Modern Prometheus.*

    Did William Shakespeare write *Twelfth Night: Or What You Will*?

Activity

Place colons where they are needed within these sentences.

A. Please bring the following items with you watch, ring, cell phone, and pen.

B. Dear Madam (as the salutation of a business letter)

C. The following students have been selected for the varsity debate team Matthew, Hillary, and Sophia.

D. My grandfather saw the movie *Superman The Movie* in 1979.

E. Were you there at 440 that afternoon?

155 the semicolon

1. Use a semicolon to join two independent clauses. In this case, a conjunction is unnecessary. The two independent clauses should be closely related.

   Isaac is a champion discus thrower; he holds the state record. (This is an *acceptable* use of the semicolon.)

   Isaac is a champion discus thrower; his dad is a baker. (This is an *unacceptable* use of the semicolon.)

   The concert was not just good; it was fantastic! (This is *acceptable*.)

2. Use a semicolon between a compound sentence's clauses that are joined by certain transitional words. Use a comma after these transitional words and phrases. See the sample sentences below.

accordingly	in other words
as a result	indeed
besides	instead
consequently	meanwhile
for example	moreover
for instance	nevertheless
furthermore	otherwise
however	that is
in fact	therefore

   The new tools are great; besides, they were perfect gifts for Dad.

   Your dance score was one of the highest in this early competition; consequently, you will now move on to the next round.

3. Use a semicolon between items in a series—if the items in that series contain commas.

   This movie's special people include Missy Swit, lead; Kate Lewis, director; Morty Mulis, producer; and Freida Ling, cinematographer.

4. To eliminate confusion, use a semicolon before the coordinating conjunction that joins two independent clauses.

   At the beach we collected shells, wood, and seaweed; and then we barbequed, walked the shore, and made a campfire.

160

156 colons and semicolons in context

Insert any colon or semicolon where needed. The other marks of punctuation are correctly placed in these sentences.

1. Harriet loved to go to the shore her brother really enjoyed going with her.

2. The boater was speeding around the lake for two hours in fact, he was starting to annoy the people on the beach.

3. My great-grandfather's favorite movies include the following *Vacation*, starring Chevy Chase *One Flew Over the Cuckoo's Nest*, starring Jack Nicholson and *Funny Girl*, starring Barbra Streisand.

4. Our fitness instructor recommends these healthy foods carrots, peanuts, apples, grapes, and celery.

5. Let us plan to meet at 110 on the train platform.

6. (The secretary started her business letter with the following words)

   Dear General McNamee

   We would like to invite you . . .

7. The author told the audience members that she plans to entitle her next book *Surfing A Sport Like No Others*.

8. Our tour guide offered the group trips to these places Juneau, the capital of Alaska St. Louis, the Gateway to the West and San Francisco, the City by the Bay.

9. We need to reach our goal of $10,000 in two weeks therefore we will step up our phone campaign starting tomorrow.

10. The nurse spent much time with that one patient as a result, her time spent with the next few patients will be reduced.

157 quotation marks (part one)

When working with quotation marks (" "), follow these rules. This is the first of three pages about quotation marks.

① Use quotation marks before and directly after a speaker's exact words.

> The lifeguard told the swimmers, "Please move down between the green flags."

Note: Use a comma to separate the speaker's exact words from the sentence's other parts.

> "Please move down between the green flags," the lifeguard told the swimmers.

Note: You do not have to use quotation marks around an indirect quotation.

> The lifeguard told the beachgoers to move between the green flags if they wanted to go into the water.

Note: A direct quotation usually begins with a capital letter. If the quotation is not in its entirety, it often begins with a lowercase letter.

> Mikki believes that "honesty is its own reward."

② If a direct quotation that is a full sentence is broken up into two parts because the speaker is identified, the second part begins with a lowercase letter.

> "Since the flowers are starting to bloom," said Chris, "we should not step into the garden."

Note: If the second part of a direct quotation is a complete sentence, start that part with a capital letter. Insert a period after the unquoted portion.

> "This is beautiful!" responded Mrs. Alsager. "Keep it going!"

Note: If a person's exact words are more than a single sentence and are not divided, use only a single set of quotation marks.

> "Waves gently lapped the shore. Children played in the sand," the man reported.

158 quotation marks (part two)

This is the second of three pages dealing with quotation marks. Know these rules and include them in your writing.

③ Use a question mark or an exclamation mark within the closing quotation mark if the question mark or the exclamation mark is part of the quotation.

> "Is this the correct tool?" the assistant asked the machinist.
>
> The soldier screamed to his comrade, "Move away now!"

Note: If a question mark or an exclamation mark is a part of the whole sentence (and not just a part of the direct quotation), place the mark outside the quotation marks.

> Did Mr. Boland say, "You have only two choices left"? (The entire sentence, not the quotation, is a question.)
>
> I was so ecstatic when Jenny said, "You are our choice for class rep"! (The entire sentence, not the quotation, is the exclamation.)

④ Use a comma, exclamation mark, or question mark to separate the direct quotation from the rest of the sentence. A period cannot do the same.

> "Please help me lift this rug," Mom requested Roberta.
>
> "This is absolutely awesome!" the captain told her crew.
>
> "Will it be sunny tomorrow?" the news anchor asked her staff.

⑤ Place colons and semicolons outside the closing quotation mark.

> There are two main characters in O. Henry's story "The Gift of the Magi": Jim and Della.
>
> Karen remarked, "These two cars are full of supplies for the picnic"; only then did we realize that there was no room for any additional passengers.

159 quotation marks (part three)

This is the third of three pages dealing with quotation marks. Study these rules, and use them in your writing.

⑥ When you are writing dialogue, start a new paragraph each time the speaker changes.

> "We need to remodel the upstairs bathroom," Mom said to Dad.
>
> He asked her, "How much do you think that this job will cost us? I think that I will probably be able to do most of the work."
>
> "Great!" Mom replied. "Let's talk about the project again tomorrow."

⑦ Use only the opening quotation marks at the beginning of each paragraph when you are quoting a passage of more than one paragraph. The only time to include the closing quotation marks is at the end of the concluding paragraph.

> "The bridge was built after the immigrants began to come into the burgeoning city in large numbers. This bridge was not a luxury; it was a necessity. People demanded it, and the politicians responded quickly to their demands.
>
> "Then the good times for construction workers began—and continued—for the next three decades. There was always work— and plenty of it. To be able to use a saw and hammer meant that you were able to feed your family."

⑧ Use quotation marks to enclose the titles of the following: chapters, songs, articles, short poems, and short stories.

> "Before Hitting the Water" (chapter) from *Kayaking for Fitness*
>
> "America the Beautiful" (song)
>
> "More Strain, More Injuries" (article)
>
> "Stopping by Woods on a Snowy Evening" (short poem)
>
> "Beware of the Dog" (short story)

160 italics, hyphens, and brackets

① Use *italics* (or an <u>underline</u>) for the titles of the following:

books (*Brain Games*)

comic strips (*Pogo*)

full-length plays (*The Crucible*)

long poems (*The Aeneid*)

magazines (*Sports Illustrated*)

movies (*The Sound of Music*)

newspapers (*New York Times*)

ships and planes (U.S.S. *Constitution, The Spirit of St. Louis*)

television and radio programs (*Law and Order, All Things Considered*)

works of art (*Pietà*)

② Use a *hyphen*

- to syllabicate words at the end of a line of typing or writing. Divide words of two or more syllables ONLY between syllables. Do not divide single-syllable words.

- to separate portions of certain compound nouns, such as *father-in-law* and *editor-in-chief*.

- between two words that comprise a single adjective (only when these words precede the noun that they are describing). Examples include *moth-infected* clothing and *rosy-cheeked* elf.

Note: If a word that comprises a single adjective ends with *-ly*, a hyphen is not necessary. (The *rudely* behaved spectator was spoken to by the usher.)

③ Use *brackets* to enclose explanations, comments, or a correction *within quoted or parenthetical material*.

The reporter told the audience, "The New York Mets' first world championship [1969] was memorable for all New Yorkers."

William Shakespeare (known as the Bard of Avon [1564–1616]) wrote many comedies, histories, and tragedies.

161 parentheses, ellipsis marks, and dashes

Use the following rules for these three punctuation marks.

① *Parentheses* **( )** are used to

- enclose numbers or letters in a series within a sentence

    There are three different types of learners: (1) visual, (2) auditory, and (3) tactile-kinesthetic.

- enclose extra materials

    Priscilla Smith (née Franklin) is a talented orator.

    Marla's favorite U.S. president, John F. Kennedy (1961–1963), was our nation's thirty-fifth President.

- enclose explanatory materials

    Her first year in office (2009) was a busy one indeed.

② *Ellipsis marks* **(. . .)** are used to

- indicate that material has been omitted from a quotation

    "The best that has happened . . . was all due to your efforts," Michaela proudly told her brother, Nico.

- indicate that a statement or series is not complete

    The rigorous examination includes essays on various topics (trade rights, antidiscrimination laws, . . .) that challenge all of the law students.

③ A *dash* **(—)** is used to

- indicate a sudden break in the sentence

    That was a hard fact to believe—even for the most cynical among us.

- indicate an interruption in speech

    "Well—um—I just thought that the plan would work," the embarrassed boy told his parents.

- highlight or explain a word or series of words in a sentence

    These excellent singers—Mike, Joan, Terri, and Marcia—will continue to work here at the resort for as long as they want.

Activity

Insert the necessary punctuation where needed.

1. Will you please hand me that wrench asked Jimmy Bevy

2. She replied You can contribute any amount that you can afford We accept all donations

3. They will find Rex went on that this meal is very tasty

4. The rancher said to her assistants We need to move this herd before the storm arrives Lets get to it immediately

5. We swam thirty laps yesterday Ricardo stated We will swim an additional twenty laps this morning

6. I have never met a man Nicky said whom I respected more

7. Look out Here comes that vicious dog Mr Boyle warned his children

8. Did Ms Wright say Yvonne can do no wrong

9. Laverne screamed Youre going to knock over that expensive vase Betty

10. Can you take this heavy package to Tom Ted asked Tim You will need your car to haul it

163 All the punctuation is missing!

Activity

All of the punctuation marks in these ten sentences are missing. Insert whatever punctuation (apostrophe, comma, colon, semicolon, quotation marks, italics, hyphen, brackets, parentheses, ellipsis marks, and dash) is needed to make these sentences flow better. Each mark of punctuation is used at least once. Retain all of the original words.

1. Have you seen Rocky featuring Sylvester Stallone Lucy asked Malik

2. There are several genres of literature that we will study here in college this semester 1 short stories 2 novels 3 poems and 4 plays

3. The year Alfredo was born 1996 was the same year that his dad graduated from medical school

4. Many subjects physics, English, civics...challenge students to work diligently

5. These mummies have been in the museum for many years in fact they have been here since the museum's inception

6. Please bring these items to the work site this morning hammer chisel drill and saw

7. Miguels hat was found near the malls main office

8. May I ask your sister in law to dance Ronaldo asked Paula

9. "I um think that well you can come with us now the shy manager informed Rita

10. The conventioneers told of their 1967 actually 1968 summer experiences in Chicago that summer the professor informed her students

164 first capitalization list

Here are names of people, places, and things to capitalize. This is the first of two lists of names that require capital letters.

Albums (*Abbey Road*, *Grease*)
Awards (Emmys®, Oscars®)
Bodies of water (Atlantic Ocean, Lake Superior)
Books (*The Adventures of Tom Sawyer*, the *Bible*)
Buildings and other structures (the Taj Mahal, Empire State Building)
Businesses (Moe's Greeting Cards, Tom's Beverage)
Car models (Toyota Camry, Nissan Sentra)
CD's (*Nannie's Tunes*, *Three Famous Composers*)
Chapters and other parts of a book ("My Life," "Soccer")
Cities (Fresno, Tallahassee)
Comic strips (*Peanuts*, *For Better or Worse*)
Computer programs (Microsoft Word, Excel)
Constellations (Aquarius, Libra)
Continents (Africa, Asia)
Counties (Norfolk, Dade)
Countries (Spain, Ireland)
Days (Thursday, Saturday)
Essays ("Self Reliance," "The Philosophy of Composition")
Family names (Uncle John, Cousin Moe)
Galaxies (Milky Way, Andromeda)
Governmental bodies (U.S. Senate, Department of the Interior)
Historical documents (Bill of Rights, U.S. Constitution)
Historical events and periods (Battle of Bunker Hill, the Renaissance)
Holidays (Labor Day, Fourth of July)
Holy days (Ramadan, Yom Kippur)
Institutions (Marquette University, City College of New York)
Islands (Aruba, Crete)
Months (January, December)
Monuments (Mount Rushmore, Lincoln Memorial)
Mountains (Rocky Mountains, Appalachian Mountains)
Movies (*Rocky*, *The Outsiders*)
Musical works (*Dark Side of the Moon, If I Were a Rich Man*)
Nationalities (Greek, Chinese)

165 second capitalization list

Here are names of people, places, and things to capitalize.

Organizations (Girl Scouts of America, American Bar Association)

Parishes (Vernon Parish, Terrebonne Parish)

Parks (Yellowstone National Park, Bryce Canyon National Park)

Periodicals (*Time*, *Newsweek*)

Planets (Saturn, Mercury)

Plays (*Death of a Salesman*, *The Master Builder*)

Poems ("Boy Wandering in Simms' Valley," "Richard Cory")

Product names (Hostess Twinkies®, Evian® water)

Races (Caucasian, Indian)

Regions (Southeast, Northwest)

Religions and their followers (Catholicism, Protestants)

Religious celebrations (Easter, Rosh Hashanah)

Roads (Lincoln Highway, US 1)

Sacred writings (*Talmud*, *Koran*)

School subjects (capitalize only languages and courses that have a number or letter after them) (English, Math A, Biology 101)

Ships (U.S.S. *Constitution*, *Monitor*)

Short stories ("The Ransom of Red Chief," "Luck")

Spacecraft (*Mir*, *Sputnik*)

Special events (Mother's Day, Oklahoma State Fair)

Stars (Pollux, Castor)

States (South Carolina, Texas)

Streets (Winters Avenue, Mansfield Drive)

Teams (San Diego Chargers, Boston Red Sox)

Television and radio programs (*Week in Review*, *Car Talk*)

Titles of people's names (Dr. Landerson, Mrs. Pennington)

Towns (Clinton, Canton)

Townships (Daggett Township, Duplain Township)

Trains (Golden Gate, Tulsan)

Video games (*Chain Reaction*, *Crossword Puzzler*)

Videos (*The History of Independence Day*, *Golfing*)

Works of art (*Pietà*, *American Gothic*)

166 using capital letters

Here are some useful capitalization rules to follow.

① Capitalize the first word of every sentence.

>Your poem was read at this morning's assembly.
>Begin the session now.

② Capitalize the pronoun *I* as a word and in a contraction.

>This card is something that I cherish.
>I've a funny story to tell you.

③ Capitalize proper nouns and proper adjectives.

>South America—South American capitals
>Italy—Italian cities
>Emerson—Emersonian ideals

④ Capitalize the first word of a quoted sentence.

>"Many surprises are awaiting you, Yogi."

⑤ Capitalize the interjection O.

>O, say can you see, by the dawn's early light . . .

⑥ Capitalize the abbreviations of proper nouns.

>Mount Rainier . . . Mt. Rainier
>Twenty-third Street . . . Twenty-third St.
>Reverend Jones . . . Rev. Jones

⑦ Capitalize the first word of the salutation and the closing of friendly and business letters.

>Dear Mrs. Lowe,
>Sincerely yours,
>Respectfully,
>Dear Madam:

167 capitalize these (part one)

 **Activity** Draw three lines beneath each letter that requires a capital letter.

1. mike's cousin lives in norwood, massachusetts.

2. will the pittsburgh penguins play the new york rangers this month?

3. is 242 northfield ave. the correct address?

4. we studied about the pacific ocean on wednesday and the atlantic ocean on friday.

5. us 10 runs through minnesota.

6. which is your sign—pisces or libra?

7. hank hall joined the boy scouts of america in november.

8. when will the members of the united states senate reconvene?

9. gino's pizza palace is in the next town.

10. when was the empire state building opened?

11. how many oscars has meryl streep won?

12. three hundred guests attended the gala labor day event thrown by uncle joe.

13. john and mary, two americans, owned wakefield beverage.

14. have you received your notes on protestantism and judaism?

15. charles lindbergh piloted *the spirit of st. louis* from new york to paris in 1927.

168 capitalize these (part two)

 **Activity** Draw three lines beneath each letter that needs to be capitalized.

1. my relatives, uncle ted and aunt flo, traveled in a boeing airplane last fall.

2. you will be intrigued by the movie *murder on the orient express*.

3. the statue of liberty is a symbol of freedom.

4. the bible and the koran are popular books.

5. miguel owns a toyota venza and a nissan ultima.

6. *pride and prejudice*, *jane eyre*, and *one flew over the cuckoo's nest* are among herb's favorite novels.

7. mathematics, social studies, french, and english were hard classes for juliet.

8. we purchased tickets for two broadway musicals, *jersey boys* and *billy elliot*.

9. chapter one, "how to be a success," is very well written.

10. this month we will read and discuss three short stories—"the gift of the magi," "the necklace," and "the open window."

11. have you seen vincent van gogh's painting "starry night," or edward hopper's painting "nighthawks"?

12. one of lisa's favorite films is *citizen kane*.

13. my sisters especially enjoy two comic strips, "archie" and "family circle."

14. aunt gina and grandpa gino visited the grand canyon last october.

15. yvonne attended cornell university in ithaca, new york.

169 challenging spelling words

Here are over 150 challenging spelling words that you should study and use. In addition, look up the meaning of any word that is not familiar to you.

absence	curiosity	ideally	nickel	seize
acceptable	defendant	immature	niece	separate
accidentally	definite	immigrate	noisy	sergeant
accommodate	dilemma	interfere	nominal	sizable
acquaint	disappear	interrupt	nonentity	success
acquire	disaster	irregular	occasion	symbolize
aerial	discipline	jaunty	occurred	symmetry
already	eighth	jealous	occurrence	tendency
amateur	emigrate	justification	omnipotent	thief
analysis	emphasis	knowledge	operable	thorough
analyze	emphasize	kowtow	paradigm	through
apparent	exceed	liberal	parallel	thwart
appearance	excessive	license	permanent	tonal
argument	existence	likelihood	personal	tragedy
assistance	flabbergast	loneliness	personnel	truly
belief	foreign	lonely	persuasive	unified
believe	fractious	loveable	pitiful	unique
benefit	fragile	luxury	possess	unnecessary
bureau	gauge	mammoth	prejudice	usually
business	genuine	manageable	privilege	vicious
calendar	grammar	manipulate	psychology	villain
catastrophe	grateful	marriage	pursuit	violin
category	gratitude	mileage	receipt	weight
cemetery	grisly	miniscule	receive	weird
changeable	guarantee	miserable	recommend	wield
column	guilty	misspell	regrettable	willful
committed	handkerchief	mortgage	reliable	yield
condemn	height	municipal	reliance	zany
conscience	heiress	muscle	resolution	zealous
conscious	humane	neighbor	rhythm	
courageous	icicle	niceties	secede	

170 spell it right—and win the battle

On the line provided, write the corresponding letter of the correctly spelled word in each pair. Then write those twenty letters, in order, on the line beneath the last pair of words. If your letters are correct, you will spell out a word that helps this activity's title make sense.

1. _____	(b) unecessary	(c) unnecessary
2. _____	(o) immigrate	(p) imigrate
3. _____	(u) icicle	(v) iceikle
4. _____	(m) minascule	(n) miniscule
5. _____	(s) apparant	(t) apparent
6. _____	(e) heiress	(f) hearess
7. _____	(r) knowledge	(s) knowlidge
8. _____	(p) existance	(r) existence
9. _____	(d) comitted	(e) committed
10. _____	(v) foreign	(w) foriegn
11. _____	(n) analize	(o) analyze
12. _____	(l) genuine	(m) genuinne
13. _____	(t) tendoncy	(u) tendency
14. _____	(s) predjudice	(t) prejudice
15. _____	(h) dilema	(i) dilemma
16. _____	(o) assistance	(p) assistence
17. _____	(n) occurrence	(o) occurence
18. _____	(a) misspell	(b) mispell
19. _____	(r) interrupt	(s) interupt
20. _____	(x) morgage	(y) mortgage

The twenty-letter word is _____.

SECTION FOUR

Show What You Know

171 Where did all the letters go?

Activity

Each spelling word is missing one or more letters. Use the spaces provided to fill in the letters.

1. m i l e __ g e
2. i __ __ e g u l a r
3. c o l u m __
4. a c c o m __ o d a t e
5. h e i g __ t
6. u n __ e c e s s a r y
7. v i l l __ i n
8. n __ __ g h b o r
9. r e g r e __ __ a b l e
10. o c c u r r __ n c e
11. s __ __ z e
12. o __ __ a s i o n
13. t h o r __ __ g h
14. p a r a d i __ m
15. n i c __ e l
16. m i n __ s c u l e
17. m a n a g __ a b l e
18. t h __ e f
19. p a r __ l l e l
20. c e m __ t __ r y

21. a m a t __ __ r
22. a __ q u i r e
23. h __ __ r e s s
24. e x i s t __ n c e
25. b e l __ __ v e
26. w i __ l d
27. w e __ r d
28. s __ r g e a n t
29. p r e __ u d i c e
30. c o n s __ i o u s
31. a p p a r __ n t
32. m o r __ g a g e
33. c o n d e m __
34. g r a m m __ r
35. c a l e n d __ r
36. b e n __ f i t
37. g e n u __ n e
38. l i c e n __ e
39. d i s __ i p l i n e
40. f o r e __ g n

172 grammar and *Twenty Thousand Leagues Under the Sea*

Activity

Here is the opening passage from *Twenty Thousand Leagues Under the Sea*, a novel by Jules Verne. Each sentence's number appears in parentheses before the sentence. Answer the questions on the lines provided for you.

(1) The year 1866 was marked by a bizarre development, an unexplained and downright inexplicable phenomenon that surely no one has forgotten. (2) Without getting into those rumors that upset civilians in the seaports and deranged the public mind even far inland, it must be said that professional seamen were especially alarmed. (3) Traders, ship owners, captains of vessels, skippers, and master mariners from Europe and America, naval officers from every country, and at their heels the various national governments on these two continents, were all extremely disturbed by the business.

1. Name the two verb phrases in the first sentence. _____ and _____

2. What part of speech is *especially* in sentence two? _____

3. Why are there commas in between the first few words of sentence three? _____

4. Name three adjectives in the first sentence. _____, _____, and _____

5. What word in the second sentence is acting as both an adjective and a pronoun? _____

6. Is the prepositional phrase, *on these two continents*, in the third sentence, an adjective or an adverb phrase? _____

7. The noun clause in the second sentence is _____

_____.

173 grammar, mechanics, and *Alice in Wonderland*

Activity

Here are ten questions about grammar and mechanics in this one-sentence passage from Lewis Carroll's book, *Alice in Wonderland.* Answer the questions on the lines provided. The four sections of the text are numbered in parentheses after each section.

Alice was beginning to get very tired of sitting by her sister on the bank, and (1) of having nothing to do: once or twice she had peeped into the book her sister (2) was reading, but it had no pictures or conversations in it, "and what is the use (3) of a book," thought Alice, "without pictures or conversations?" (4)

1. Name a proper noun in the first section of text. _____

2. What is the conjunction in the first section of text? _____

3. Is the prepositional phrase, *by her sister*, in the first section, an adjective or an adverb phrase? (Circle one)

4. What is the infinitive in the second section of text? _____

5. What is the verb phrase in the second section of text? _____

6. *Once* and *twice*, found in the second section of text, are both what part of speech? _____

7. Name the three conjunctions in the third section of text.
   _____, _____, and _____

8. *Use*, in the third section, is what part of speech? _____

9. Why is there a comma after *book* in the fourth section?

   _____

   _____

10. Why is the question mark inside the quotation marks in the last part of the fourth section of text? _____

180

174 phrases, clauses, and sentences found in "One Thousand Dollars"

 **Activity**

Using this selection from O. Henry's short story, "One Thousand Dollars," answer each question. The passage has been broken up into Sections A, B, and C.

(Section A) "One thousand dollars," repeated Lawyer Tolman solemnly and severely, "and here is the money."

(Section B) Young Gillan gave a decidedly amused laugh as he fingered the thin package of new fifty-dollar notes.

(Section C) "It's such a confoundedly awkward amount," he explained, genially, to the lawyer. "If it had been ten thousand a fellow might wind up with a lot of fireworks and do himself credit. Even fifty dollars would have been less trouble."

① The word *repeated* in the first section is written in what tense?

_____

② In Section A, *solemnly* and *severely* are both what part of speech?

_____

③ Is the sentence in Section B, a simple, compound, or complex sentence? (Circle one)

④ What is the subordinating conjunction in Section B's sentence?

_____

⑤ Name the adjective phrase in Section B. _____

⑥ What word does *genially* describe in Section C? _____

⑦ Section C's sentence, "It's such a confoundedly awkward amount," is a simple, compound, or complex sentence? (Circle one)

⑧ Section C's sentence that begins with *If* and ends with *credit*, is a compound, complex, or compound-complex sentence? (Circle one)

⑨ Name the verb phrase in the last sentence of Section C.

_____

⑩ What is the antecedent of the pronoun *himself* in Section C?

_____

175 find the mistake

Each sentence has one mistake. On the line before the sentence, write the corresponding letter of the underlined portion (A, B, or C) that contains the error.

1. ____ None of these folders <u>has</u> (A) your signature <u>or</u> (B) your address, (C) Mike.

2. ____ "This <u>mornings'</u> (A) newspaper <u>was delivered</u> (B) at seven o'clock," (C) I told George.

3. ____ "<u>Some</u> (A) of those grass clippings were <u>taking</u> (B) to the dump by the sanitation workers," (C) Thelma told Louise.

4. ____ The gift, a shell from the Atlantic <u>Ocean,</u> (A) was given to <u>she and me</u> (B) during <u>their</u> (C) party.

5. ____ Joanna <u>borrowed</u> (A) me a book <u>that</u> (B) she had <u>already</u> (C) read.

6. ____ Many of us had <u>rode</u> (A) down that path that <u>you and I</u> (B) scouted several weeks <u>ago</u> (C).

7. ____ Our local department <u>store's</u> (A) <u>childrens'</u> (B) section is staffed by friendly <u>ladies</u> (C).

8. ____ <u>Me and Terry</u> (A) <u>gave</u> (B) them over two hundred <u>dollars' worth</u> (C) of clothing.

9. ____ <u>Someone</u> (A) said that <u>Leroy's uniform</u> (B) <u>shrinked</u> (C) after Mom had placed it in the dryer.

10. ____ "I think," (A) Justin remarked to Jonah, (B) "that they will stay at the picnic with the <u>other's</u>." (C)

176 five questions in five minutes (parts of speech, prepositional phrases, and clauses)

Activity

On the lines provided, answer these five questions in five minutes.

1. What part of speech joins words or groups of words? _____

2. Explain how a pronoun can be just a pronoun and how it can be a pronoun-adjective.

   _____

   _____

   _____

   _____

   _____

3. Using the same prepositional phrase in two different sentences, show how it can be an adjective phrase as well as an adverb phrase.

   _____

   _____

   _____

   _____

4. Which of the following clauses cannot start a sentence—adjective, adverb, or noun? Circle your answer.

5. *Down* can be used as how many different parts of speech? List them.

   _____

177 five questions in five minutes (sentences and usage)

Activity

Circle the correct answers within five minutes. Get ready. Go!

1. Which sentence is a complex sentence?
   a. The maintenance worker, and her supervisor attended the meeting.
   b. While Rome burned, Nero fiddled.
   c. The man washed his car that was in the driveway, and his wife mowed the lawn.

2. Which sentence is a compound sentence?
   a. Are you going to the show with the rest of the class members?
   b. If you can pick the correct number, you will win a trip to Europe.
   c. My mom is tall, and my dad is strong.

3. What is the past participle of the verb *bring*?
   a. brang
   b. brought
   c. brung

4. Is the subject-verb agreement correct in this sentence? Most of the garbage pails has been emptied already.
   a. Yes
   b. No

5. Circle all the words that are irregular verbs.

   a. talk
   b. grow
   c. find
   d. smell
   e. run
   f. win
   g. laugh
   h. remember
   i. sit
   j. teach

178 five questions in five minutes (mechanics)

Activity

Circle the correct answers in five minutes. A question can have more than a single answer. Ready? Go!

1 Circle all those that should be in quotation marks.

    a. song titles

    b. titles of book chapters

    c. short story titles

    d. titles of magazine articles

    e. titles of short poems

2 Capital letters should be used for which of these?

    a. titles of novels

    b. names of the seasons

    c. days of the week

    d. names of planets

    e. proper adjectives

3 Which sentences illustrate the correct use of the comma?

    a. Because the weather is nasty, the young students must stay indoors.

    b. In my opinion, this method has more benefits than the other ones.

    c. He went home to Louisiana, after that.

4 Which words are spelled correctly?

    a. iregular

    b. villian

    c. occasion

    d. apparent

5 Which answers illustrate the correct use of the apostrophe?

    a. *Helen's bike*—for the bike that belongs to Helen

    b. *the children's book*—for the book that is designed for children

    c. *Sue and Charley's house*—for the house that is co-owned by Sue and Charley

    d. *the senator's proposal*—for the proposal that the senators made together

Activity

Answer all of these questions within five minutes. Circle the answers. There may be more than one answer for any of these questions. Get set? Go!

1. Which verbal ends in *-ing* and acts like a noun?

   a. gerund

   b. infinitive

   c. participle

2. The underlined words in the sentence, *"To win the art contest was Melissa's goal,"* form what type of verbal phrase?

   a. gerund

   b. infinitive

   c. participle

3. Which sentence contains an underlined predicate nominative?

   a. Louis felt <u>uneasy</u> at the debate.

   b. Nancy was <u>intelligent</u>.

   c. Kyle was the <u>captain</u>.

4. Which sentence contains both a direct and an indirect object?

   a. When the singer entertains her audiences, the crowds applaud enthusiastically.

   b. The bluegrass fiddler gave his wife a new car.

   c. Most of these riddles can be solved if you really think about it.

5. Which sentence contains an underlined complete subject?

   a. Without <u>his trusty friend by his side</u>, Pete seemed lost.

   b. <u>The intelligent officer</u> made a wise decision in an instant.

   c. <u>Walking into the crowded train station</u>, the passenger searched for the right track.

180 five questions in five minutes (confusing and sound-alike words)

Activity

Answer these five questions within five minutes. Circle the correct answers or write your responses on the lines provided. Ready? Go!

1. Show you know the difference between the sound-alike words *quiet* and *quite* by writing two illustrative sentences, one including the word *quiet* and the other including the word *quite*.

   _____

   _____

   _____

   _____

2. Which word would you use for the outdoor conditions—*weather* or *whether*?

3. Is the word *principal* used correctly in the sentence, *The principal export of that country is coffee*? _____Yes _____ No

4. Which word—affect, effect—can be used as both a *verb* and a *noun*?

5. Show you know the difference between the often confused words *cite* and *site* by writing two illustrative sentences, one including the word *cite*, and the other including the word *site*.

   _____

   _____

   _____

   _____

ANSWER KEY

Section One: Grammar

1. The Noun

1. Rose, pet, office
2. newspaper, table, classroom
3. group, hours, plan
4. Joshua, bridge, lighthouse
5. computer, technician, Tuesday

5. Do You Know Your Personal Pronouns?

1. We
2. her
3. I
4. her
5. yours
6. they
7. Theirs
8. him
9. mine
10. him
11. Our
12. us
13. We and they
14. us
15. she, you

6. Reflexive, Demonstrative, and Interrogative Pronouns

1. Who (INT), this (DEM), herself (REF)
2. those (DEM), yourself (REF)
3. Whom (INT), these (DEM)

7. Singular and Plural Nouns and Pronouns

The singular nouns or pronouns are in numbers 1, 5, 6, 7, 9, 13, 15, 16, 18, and 20.

The plural nouns or pronouns are in numbers 2, 3, 4, 8, 10, 11, 12, 14, 17, and 19.

8. The Adjective

(Answers will vary.)

11. Is It an Action, Linking, or Helping Verb?

Sentences 4, 6, 7, 10, and 11 include action verbs.

Sentences 1, 5, 8, 12, and 13 include linking verbs.

Sentences 2, 3, 9, 14, and 15 include helping verbs.

15. The Coordinating Conjunction

1 for   **2** yet   **3** but   **4** or   **5** so

16. The Correlative Conjunction

(These are possible answers.)

1 Whether ... or

2 Either ... or; Both ... and; Neither ... nor

3 both ... and; either ... or; neither ... nor

4 neither ... nor

5 Not only ... but also

17. The Subordinating Conjunction

(These are possible answers. There could be others.)

1 since   **2** as if   **3** when   **4** Unless   **5** whenever

18. Combining Ideas with the Subordinating Conjunction

(These are possible answers. There could be others.)

1 When the bell rang, the students moved to the next period.

2 Unless you finish your science project, you cannot play your video game.

3 We were watching the nightly news when we received a phone call from my aunt.

4 My cat, Belinda, started to hiss when the veterinarian approached.

⑤ You will want to try an even harder puzzle after you solve this challenging puzzle.

⑥ Stand here while I take your picture.

⑦ If Johann gets a ride, he will go to the concert.

⑧ François explored the surroundings as his friends asked him questions.

⑨ The garbage cans were left out in the street after the garbage collectors emptied the cans in the early morning.

⑩ My brother, Eduardo, turned pale when he saw a ghost.

19. The Interjection

(Answers will vary.)

20. Parts-of-Speech Review (Part One)

Nouns are found in sentences 1, 3, 10, 17, and 18.

A pronoun is found in sentence 6.

Adjectives are found in sentences 5, 12, 15, and 20.

Verbs are found in sentences 2, 11, 16, and 19.

Adverbs are found in sentences 4 and 13.

Prepositions are found in sentences 8 and 14.

A conjunction is found in sentence 9.

An interjection is found in sentence 7.

21. Parts-of-Speech Review (Part Two)

Nouns are found in sentences 1, 8, and 16.

Pronouns are found in sentences 5, 14, and 20.

Adjectives are found in sentences 12 and 18.

Verbs are found in sentences 4, 7, and 17.

Adverbs are found in sentences 2, 3, and 15.

Prepositions are found in sentences 6 and 11.

Conjunctions are found in sentences 9, 10, and 19.

An interjection is found in sentence 13.

 Answer Key

22. Parts-of-Speech Parade

(These are possible answers.)

① This <u>part</u> of the trip is easy.

② We must <u>part</u> now, but we shall see each other again very soon.

③ The network <u>televised</u> three presidential debates that year.

④ This Olympic match will be a <u>televised</u> event.

⑤ <u>Lower</u> this crate carefully.

⑥ This <u>lower</u> electric outlet is better.

⑦ I cannot go <u>for</u> I must sit with my younger siblings.

⑧ Manny grabbed <u>for</u> the ring during the carousel ride.

⑨ <u>Before</u> you go, please give me your phone number.

⑩ George stood <u>before</u> the crowd.

23. Filling in the Parts of Speech

① adjective (adj)

② conjunction (c)

③ pronoun (pro)

④ interjection (int)

⑤ preposition (prep)

⑥ adverb (advb)

⑦ verb (v)

⑧ noun (n)

⑨ pronoun (pro)

⑩ preposition (prep)

⑪ adjective (adj)

⑫ conjunction (c)

⑬ adjective (adj)

⑭ verb (v)

⑮ adverb (advb)

24. What's Missing? (Parts-of-Speech Review)

Nouns are found in sentences 8 and 13.

A pronoun is found in sentence 3.

Adjectives are found in sentences 5, 11, and 12.

Verbs are found in sentences 9, 14, and 15.

An adverb is found in sentence 1.

Prepositions are found in sentences 4 and 10.

Conjunctions are found in sentences 2 and 7.

An interjection is found in sentence 6.

25. Fun with Literary Titles (Parts-of-Speech Review)

Nouns are underlined in titles 3, 10, 13, and 16.

Pronouns are underlined in titles 11 (pronoun/adjective) and 18.

Verbs are underlined in titles 1 and 6.

Adjectives are underlined in titles 4, 5, 9, 11 (pronoun/adjective), 12, 14, and 17.

Prepositions are underlined in titles 2, 8, 19, and 20.

Conjunctions are underlined in titles 7 and 15.

(There are no adverbs or interjections.)

26. Parts-of-Speech Matching

① D   ④ O   ⑦ I   ⑩ C   ⑬ A

② F   ⑤ E   ⑧ N   ⑪ J   ⑭ H

③ K   ⑥ B   ⑨ M   ⑫ L   ⑮ G

Section Two: Usage

27. Complete and Simple Subjects

① *Complete subject:* Threatening skies; *Simple subject:* skies

② *Complete subject:* Many engineers from neighboring communities; *Simple subject:* engineers

③ *Complete subject:* Huge trucks; *Simple subject:* trucks

④ *Complete subject:* The Padres; *Simple subject:* Padres

⑤ *Complete subject:* The talented actress; *Simple subject:* actress

28. Complete and Simple Predicates

① *Complete predicate:* heard the blaring sirens; *Simple predicate:* heard

② *Complete predicate:* were crying during the awards ceremony; *Simple predicate:* were crying

③ *Complete predicate:* give their best efforts all the time; *Simple predicate:* give

④ *Complete predicate:* yelled at the speeding motorist; *Simple predicate:* yelled

⑤ *Complete predicate:* will be chosen as this year's recipient; *Simple predicate:* will be chosen

30. The Direct Object

1. brother
2. sign
3. sting
4. string
5. wager
6. beet
7. sweater

31. The Indirect Object

1. *Indirect object:* her; *Direct object:* compliment
2. *Indirect object:* me; *Direct object:* money
3. *Indirect object:* Mom; *Direct object:* dinner
4. *Indirect object:* you; *Direct object:* newspaper
5. *Indirect object:* her; *Direct object:* secret

32. The Object of the Preposition

(The prepositional phrase is given and the object or objects of the preposition are underlined.)

1. for the *trip*
2. for the *occasion*
3. to their *home*
4. without *me*
5. from *China*
6. after *dinner*
7. by community *volunteers*
8. of the *puppets*
9. by *Christina* and *Carla*
10. for *you* and *Moe*

33. Objects and 8–7–5

The direct objects are found in sentences 1, 5, 8, 10, 14, 17, 18, and 20.

The indirect objects are found in sentences 2, 6, 12, 13, 15, 16, and 19.

The objects of the preposition are found in sentences 3, 4, 7, 9, and 11.

34. Subject Complements—Predicate Nominatives and Predicate Adjectives

(Answers will vary.)

35. Predicate Nominative, Predicate Adjective, or Neither?

The predicate nominatives are in sentences 1, 4, 12, 13, and 15.

The predicate adjectives are in sentences 2, 5, 7, 8, and 9.

There are no predicate nominatives or predicate adjectives in sentences 3, 6, 10, 11, and 14.

37. The Verb Phrase

(Answers will vary.)

38. The Prepositional Phrase

(The italicized word is the object of the preposition.)

1. without *him*
2. throughout the *neighborhood*
3. Beyond the *river*
4. of the *sailors*; aboard the *ship*
5. In the *meantime*
6. in her *backyard*
7. during the *movie*
8. with their *equipment*
9. of the *boats*; along the *river*
10. of the *women*; except *Denise*; at the *meeting*

39. The Adjective Phrase

Numbers 2 and 3 are YES; numbers 1, 4, and 5 are NO.

40. The Adverb Phrase

(These are possible answers.)

1. on Tuesday morning
2. into the living room
3. by themselves
4. after much discussion
5. In the morning

41. Adjective and Adverb Phrases' Review

Sentences 1, 4, 5, 8, 9, 11, 13, 16, 17, and 19 include adjective phrases.
Sentences 2, 3, 6, 7, 10, 12, 14, 15, 18, and 20 include adverb phrases.

42. Prepositional Phrases' Review

1. ADVB—by the maintenance workers
2. ADVB—in a few minutes
3. ADJ—to tomorrow night's concert

④ ADVB—within every sentence

⑤ ADVB—during their investigation

⑥ ADVB—in fact

⑦ ADJ—in this tank

⑧ ADVB—Without much fanfare

⑨ ADVB—in her van

⑩ ADVB—instead of something else

⑪ ADJ—with the basket

⑫ ADJ—from Hester's living room

⑬ ADVB—on duty

⑭ ADVB—near our house

⑮ ADVB—with both hands

⑯ ADVB—in the bay

⑰ ADJ—in the ocean

⑱ ADVB—for a very long time

⑲ ADJ—of surprise

⑳ ADVB—into the heavens

43. The Appositive

(Answers will vary.)

44. Appositive, Verb, or Prepositional Phrase?

Sentences 2, 7, 8, 9, and 14 include appositive phrases.

Sentences 1, 5, 6, 10, and 12 include verb phrases.

Sentences 3, 4, 11, 13, and 15 include prepositional phrases.

46. Participial Phrase or Not?

Sentences 2, 3, 6, 8, 9, 12, 13, and 14 contain participial phrases.

Sentences 1, 4, 5, 7, 10, 11, and 15 do not contain participial phrases.

48. Gerund or Not?

Sentences 2, 4, 5, 6, 7, 9, 10, 12, 13, and 14 contain gerund phrases.

50. The Many Uses of the Infinitive Phrase

(1) ADVB—to meet his brother

(2) N—to revisit Europe

(3) N—To collect the entire series of presidential cards

(4) ADVB—to display their artwork

(5) ADJ—to teach well

(6) N—to listen to Broadway tunes

(7) ADVB—to buy some Italian hero sandwiches

(8) ADJ—to invite to the ceremony

(9) N—to call you last night

(10) ADVB—to participate in the contest

(11) ADJ—to improve your performance

(12) ADJ—to hold the musical instrument

(13) ADJ—to memorize the poem

(14) ADVB—to find the correct answer

(15) N—To do all of her illustrations well

51. Verbal Phrase Review

(1) P—helping the English 11 students

(2) I—to introduce the contestants

(3) I—To learn the Greek alphabet

(4) G—Participating in the Indy 500 this year

(5) G—drawing on the board

(6) P—Skateboarding most of the morning

(7) I—to watch

(8) P—Knowing how to get back to its nest

(9) G—Watching the bathers swim

(10) P—recognizing his mistakes

(11) G—Running after his kite

(12) G—Talking on the cell phone

(13) I—to catch the taxi

(14) P—held in New York City

(15) I—to win his town's art contest

52. Matching the Phrases in Context

Selection One
(1) D   (2) C   (3) B   (4) A   (5) E   (6) F   (7) G

Selection Two
(1) E   (2) G   (3) F   (4) D   (5) A   (6) C   (7) B

53. Showing What You Know About Phrases

(1) D   (2) C   (3) G   (4) A   (5) E   (6) F   (7) B

54. Happy in Ten Different Ways

(These are possible sentences.)

(1) We witnessed the parents' joy <u>during the happy event</u>. (prepositional phrase)

(2) The <u>happy</u> sailing instructor cheered her students on during the regatta. (adjective)

(3) <u>Staying happy</u> is not that easy for all people. (gerund phrase)

(4) <u>Happy after the victory</u>, the excited participant hugged her teammates. (participial phrase)

(5) Steve chose <u>to remain happy</u> even during the most challenging days and nights. (infinitive phrase)

(6) Joe Burderi, <u>the happy photographer</u>, warmly greeted the students before the shoot. (appositive phrase)

(7) These merchants were <u>happy</u> while the customers shopped in their stores. (predicate adjective)

(8) <u>Happy</u> is an adjective. (subject of the sentence)

(9) The woman <u>with the happy children</u> is Vera's aunt. (adjective phrase)

(10) The hostess was <u>in a happy mood</u> during the show's taping. (adverb phrase)

55. Writing with Variety

(These are possible answers.)

1. The dolphin <u>in the larger pool</u> amazed the children with his antics.
2. The dolphin was <u>in the larger pool</u>.
3. <u>Walking across the beach</u>, the fisherman carried his bait and tackle.
4. Alex's goal is <u>to memorize the meanings of these fifty words</u>.
5. <u>Walking quickly across the beach</u> was fun for the physically fit woman.
6. Joe DiMaggio, <u>the Yankee Clipper</u>, wore number five for the New York Yankees.
7. Four aviators <u>who partook in the discussion</u> answered all of our questions.
8. <u>When the librarian ordered the books</u>, she knew they would be big hits with the children.
9. Josephine immediately knew <u>that today would be her lucky day</u>.
10. <u>In the afternoon</u> John likes to run <u>around the lake</u>.

56. Phrases Finale

Sentences 1, 3, 4, 8, 11, 12, 14, and 15 are true statements.
Sentences 2, 5, 6, 7, 9, 10, and 13 are not true statements.

58. The Adverb Clause

1. While Rome burned
2. Until the weather conditions improve
3. before we did
4. Even though Marcelle was tired
5. if you have the custodian's permission

59. Nailing Down the Adverb Clause

The adverb clauses are found in sentences 1, 2, 4, 5, 7, 8, 9, 11, 13, and 14.

61. Recognizing Adjective Clauses

(The adjective clause is listed first, the relative pronoun second, and the word that is being described by the relative pronoun last.)

1. that you will play tonight—that—instrument
2. who has sixteen home runs—who—batter
3. that your dad purchased—that—motorcycle

198   Answer Key

④ for whom this award has been named—whom—president

⑤ that you submitted—that—answers

⑥ who won last year's contest—who—Miguel

⑦ where the hide-and-seek game began last night—where—spot

⑧ which I have not watched—which—films

⑨ when most people should be getting ready for bed—when—hour

⑩ whom I have already contacted—whom—graduates

⑪ who is a very competent podiatrist—who—Dr. Gavigan

⑫ that the committee has questioned—that—proposals

⑬ that has an interesting origin—that—word

⑭ who chose to leave the session—who—Those

⑮ to whom I have told this personal information—whom—person

63. The Many Uses of the Noun Clause

Noun clauses used as subjects are underlined in sentences 3, 7, 8, and 14.

Noun clauses used as direct objects are underlined in sentences 1, 5, and 11.

Noun clauses used as indirect objects are underlined in sentences 6 and 10.

Noun clauses used as objects of the preposition are underlined in sentences 4, 12, and 13.

Noun clauses used as predicate nominatives are underlined in sentences 2, 9, and 15.

64. Adjective, Adverb, and Noun Clauses

① q	③ e	⑤ t	⑦ o	⑨ e
② u	④ s	⑥ i	⑧ n	⑩ r

The answers spell out questioner.

65. Identifying Phrases and Clauses

① C	④ D	⑦ B	⑩ H	⑬ G
② A	⑤ E	⑧ D	⑪ E	⑭ E
③ G	⑥ F	⑨ I	⑫ F	⑮ A

66. Do You Know Your Phrases and Clauses?

1. E   4. H   7. A   10. D   13. I

2. A   5. B   8. G   11. D   14. C

3. G   6. I   9. B   12. F   15. F

67. Putting Clauses into Action

(These are possible answers. There may be others.)

1. My sister, who is in the fifth grade, is tall.

2. As soon as the bell rang, three mice ran throughout the maze.

3. Last Tuesday, we visited the restaurant that is in the Sheldon Park Mall.

4. What I would like to buy are these two magazines.

5. Because Monday night's storm dropped ten inches of snow, school was canceled on Tuesday morning.

6. Whenever Lucy tells us scary ghost stories, we get frightened.

7. The deputy mayor will give whoever wins the potato sack race a blue ribbon as the prize.

69. Starting the Sentence

1. E   2. F   3. A   4. D   5. G   6. B   7. C

70. It's All About Form

1. H   3. G   5. D   7. F   9. I

2. C   4. E   6. A   8. B   10. J

72. What's What? Sentences, Fragments, and Run-On Sentences

Numbers 1, 4, 7, 11, and 15 are sentences.

Numbers 2, 5, 6, 9, and 14 are fragments.

Numbers 3, 8, 10, 12, and 13 are run-on sentences.

73. Making Sense (and Sentences)

(These are possible answers.)

1. Mount Rushmore, located in South Dakota, is fabulous.

2. Before the storm started, we moved the tables and chairs into the shed.

3. If you think that it is a workable plan, let's go with it.

4. Oliver is a great friend who never speaks badly about anybody.

5. The funny James Short just arrived.

6. My friends and I like to get wonderful exercise by skateboarding.

7. While the repairman fixed the dishwasher, we watched the documentary about Nigeria.

8. After the author wrote for seven consecutive hours, she was exhausted.

9. Looking into the car's window, the police officer spotted the evidence.

10. We like all the songs that the entertainer sang.

74. Types of Sentences by Purpose

(These are possible answers.)

I like chocolate ice cream. (declarative sentence)

Do you like vanilla ice cream? (interrogative sentence)

We won! (exclamatory sentence)

Clean the table after you have finished eating. (imperative sentence)

75. "Purposeful" Sentences

The declarative sentences are numbers 2, 6, 9, 14, and 17.

The interrogative sentences are numbers 1, 5, 11, 13, and 20.

The exclamatory sentences are numbers 8, 10, 12, 15, and 18.

The imperative sentences are numbers 3, 4, 7, 16, and 19.

77. Simple and Compound Sentences

The simple sentences are numbers 2, 5, 6, 9, and 10.

The compound sentences are numbers 1, 3, 4, 7, and 8.

78. Complex Sentences

Part One (The main clause is underlined.)

1. After his assistant arrives, <u>Van will go home</u>.

2. <u>Select a hat</u> that will block the sun well.

③ <u>Rob returned the library book</u> as soon as he found it in his locker.

④ When my pencil broke during the exam, <u>Sheila lent me hers.</u>

⑤ <u>Isaac gazed at the computer screen</u> while you were reading the schedule.

Part Two: Answers to A, B, and C will vary.

79. Compound-Complex Sentences

(These are possible insertions.)

① that my dad and uncle built

② that an operation was unnecessary

③ I look for their admirable traits

④ that we had hired; the bride looked nervous

80. Know the Sentence's Structure?

The simple sentences are numbers 2, 5, 8, and 14.
The compound sentences are numbers 1, 6, 10, and 13.
The complex sentences are numbers 3, 7, 9, 12, and 15.
The compound-complex sentences are numbers 4 and 11.

81. Subject and Verb Agreement

① drive (P)   ④ win (P)   ⑦ do (P)   ⑨ are (P)

② reads (S)   ⑤ recalls (S)   ⑧ is (S)   ⑩ were (P)

③ line (P)   ⑥ attracts (S)

83. Knowing Your Prepositional Phrases and Agreement

(The subject is listed first; the verb follows.)

① buildings—are   ⑥ persons—interest   ⑪ antiques—have

② men—were   ⑦ cans—have   ⑫ monster—frightens

③ drawing—seems   ⑧ note—was   ⑬ Several—excite

④ residents—select   ⑨ Particles—annoy   ⑭ pair—belongs

⑤ Both—are   ⑩ relative—lives   ⑮ notes—need

84. Pronouns and Their Antecedents

(The antecedent is listed first; the pronoun is listed after it.)

1. wound; itself
2. girls; their
3. Luca; he
4. Jim, Joe; they
5. cousins; they

86. Showing What You Know About Pronouns and Their Antecedents

(The antecedent is listed before its corresponding pronoun.)

1. anybody; his or her
2. none; it
3. Some; their
4. any; their
5. Neither; itself
6. Everybody; his or her
7. Several; their
8. one; his or her
9. someone; his or her
10. All; them
11. most; their
12. few; their
13. Any; their
14. Many; they
15. Each; its

88. Indefinite Pronouns and Agreement

(The number—singular or plural—is listed first; the subject is listed second; and the verb is listed last.)

1. (P) Most—pass
2. (P) None—have
3. (S) Everyone—is
4. (P) both—Do
5. (P) Several—want
6. (S) someone—Has
7. (S) Each—was
8. (P) all—Were
9. (S) More—is
10. (S) Nothing—is
11. (P) few—swim
12. (P) several—Have
13. (S) Neither—was
14. (P) Both—have
15. (S) No one—reads

89. Writing with Indefinite Pronouns

(These are possible answers.)

1. Neither of us wants to miss the concert.
2. A few of the dishes need washing.
3. Most of the puzzle has been completed.
4. Most of the tickets have been collected.

⑤ Someone in these rooms has left this package on the table.

⑥ Some of this newspaper is in the other room.

⑦ Some of the cards feel sticky.

⑧ Is any of the homework completed?

⑨ Somebody found Lester's cell phone in the locker room.

⑩ Are all of the dresses in this department on sale today?

92. Working with Compound Subjects

① was   **④** was   **⑦** occupy   **⑩** is   **⑬** were

② have   **⑤** are   **⑧** Do   **⑪** are   **⑭** are

③ are   **⑥** has   **⑨** Has   **⑫** is   **⑮** is

95. Making the Wrong Right

① One of my friends is here in this room with the rest of us.

② The pillow is too hard on my neck.

③ These oranges from Florida are juicy.

④ A few of the painters at that table have finished their work.

⑤ Before she started her workout, Lupita was listening to the broadcast.

⑥ The university officials are now admitting more students.

⑦ Proponents favor this new methodology of training doctors how to be more receptive to their patients' concerns.

⑧ Then the physician inserts (or inserted) the fluid into the other vial.

⑨ The film festival that was held in the mountains was well attended.

⑩ Concert attendees admire that singer who really knows how to entertain her audience members.

⑪ The number of graduates is higher this year.

⑫ The people in our neighborhood in Queens are very friendly.

⑬ You do not have to be at the gate that early.

⑭ Some soldiers are on our train heading for Portland, Oregon.

⑮ They do not have the winning ticket in last night's lottery.

96. Knowing Your Subject-Verb Agreement

1. are
2. indicates
3. are
4. makes
5. meet
6. has
7. leaves
8. leave
9. exchange
10. captures
11. attends
12. is
13. is
14. are
15. have
16. help
17. need
18. provides
19. attend
20. is

97. Subject-Verb Agreement Parade

1. have
2. is
3. are
4. don't
5. are
6. was
7. have
8. is
9. is
10. doesn't
11. was
12. are
13. weren't
14. are
15. has
16. are
17. is
18. is
19. are
20. has

98. Practicing Agreement

(These are possible sentences.)

1. Rick and his pals went to the city last night.
2. Most of the animals stayed in their cages during the hailstorm.
3. They forget to take their sunglasses with them.
4. Anybody who would like to go on the field trip should bring his or her money to the main office this week.
5. Physics is a very challenging class.
6. Both the girls and their brother want to go to this restaurant for dinner.
7. Herman thought that he could move the bundles by himself.
8. My favorite team is the Detroit Tigers.
9. Here is tonight's plan.
10. Either my dad or his friends are going to go fishing with us.

99. How Well Do You Know Agreement?

1. is
2. her
3. was
4. are
5. them
6. don't
7. his or her
8. are
9. are
10. need
11. is
12. is
13. has
14. is
15. was

101. Selecting the Correct Verb Tense

1. aired
2. reviewed
3. helped
4. supposed
5. needed
6. sliced
7. imagining
8. have been moved
9. invite
10. sang
11. been replaced
12. quacking
13. has been reviewing
14. had fallen
15. has been painting

103. Working with Irregular Verbs from Part One

1. came
2. drawn
3. cost
4. drunk
5. held
6. felt
7. went
8. grew
9. gotten
10. chosen
11. begun
12. found
13. fell
14. begin
15. brought

105. Working with Irregular Verbs from Part Two

1. wear
2. wrote
3. lost
4. sung
5. sent
6. spoken
7. sat
8. take
9. shrank
10. told
11. written
12. swam
13. torn
14. won
15. run

106. Irregular Verbs in Context

1. won
2. shrank
3. led
4. drawn
5. froze
6. caught
7. brought
8. began
9. gave
10. rode
11. given
12. risen
13. sank
14. driven
15. sent

107. Correct or Incorrect?

1. caught
3. sank
4. run
6. written
8. kept
9. did
11. given
15. sung

The verbs in numbers 2, 5, 7, 10, 12, 13, and 14 are correct.

108. Helping Out with Irregular Verbs

(This paragraph shows the correct irregular verbs. Other writing errors may still be present.)

Last summer, we went to the Rocky Mountains for our family vacation. On the way there, we sang many songs and kept a log of our journey. After Dad had driven three hundred miles on that first day, Mom and he decided to stop in a hotel for the afternoon and night. The hotel had an indoor swimming pool. Since last year's bathing suit had not torn or lost its color, I wore it in the hotel's pool where my brother and I swam for a while. Mom brought us some snacks and drinks that we ate and drank by the pool. I also bought some ice cream bars that I had seen in the snack shop. Later that evening, after all of us ate a good dinner, we went to our rooms to enjoy a good night's sleep.

110. Busy with the Verb "Be"

1. have
2. Were
3. are
4. Were
5. be
6. were
7. Were
8. wasn't
9. been
10. wasn't
11. was
12. been
13. are
14. are
15. Weren't
16. Is
17. were
18. Were
19. Am
20. are

111. The Nominative Case

1. S
2. PN
3. S
4. PN
5. A

114. The Possessive Case and Pronouns

(Answers will vary.)

115. Indefinite Pronouns and the Possessive Case

1. everybody
2. Somebody's
3. nobody
4. nobody else's
5. everyone's
6. Somebody else
7. somebody else
8. Anyone else's
9. Nobody's
10. Somebody else

116. Using the Possessive Case

1. Lesley's house
2. Joe and Jim's house
3. Joe's and Jim's two houses
4. that woman's car
5. the women's cars
6. a dollar's value
7. the machinists' salaries
8. my father-in-law's motorcycle
9. the committee's plan
10. the committees' plans
11. his suggestions
12. Ulysses' store
13. its address
14. Tom's bike
15. Thomas's bike

125. Matching Up the Confusing Words

1. C
2. L
3. G
4. M
5. O
6. H
7. D
8. A
9. J
10. F
11. B
12. E
13. K
14. N
15. I

126. Which Is the Correct Word?

1. Take
2. lend
3. in
4. let
5. It's
6. quotations
7. pour
8. uninterested
9. infer
10. personal
11. than
12. set
13. have
14. notorious
15. Unless

127. Select the Correct Word

1. May
2. liable
3. farther
4. beside
5. aide
6. further
7. fewer
8. immigrated to
9. scent
10. right
11. Then
12. affect
13. anywhere
14. Teach
15. rite

Part Two: The answers will vary.

128. Double Negatives

1. Linda can have no friends over tonight. **or** Linda can't have any friends over tonight.

② The nurse doesn't ever give bad health advice. **or** The nurse never gives bad health advice.

③ I hadn't noticed anybody in the room. **or** I had noticed nobody in the room.

④ This pen has no ink left in it. **or** This pen doesn't have ink left in it.

⑤ After exchanging their presents, my friends didn't do anything more to celebrate the occasion. **or** After exchanging their presents, my friends did nothing more to celebrate the occasion.

130. Revising Sentences That Have Misplaced and Dangling Modifiers

(These are possible changes.)

① To move this heavy package, you need strength.

② Walking quickly, we crossed the road.

③ Laughing loudly, Emma read the cartoon.

④ While I was washing the dishes, my cell phone rang.

⑤ Bob saw the bow glued to the present.

⑥ Looking under the bed, I spotted my birthday gift.

⑦ The car moved along the highway that extended for over three hundred miles.

⑧ I saw a star shining in the distance.

⑨ I ate my hamburger that had been wrapped in silver foil.

⑩ Driving his motorcycle, Hal noticed a kangaroo.

131. Transitive and Intransitive Verbs

The transitive verbs are in sentences 2 and 3.

The intransitive verbs are in sentences 1, 4, and 5.

132. Do You Know Your Transitive and Intransitive Verbs?

The sentences that include transitive (T) verbs are numbers 1, 3, 4, 6, 7, 8, 9, 13, 17, and 20.

The sentences that include intransitive (I) verbs are numbers 2, 5, 10, 11, 12, 14, 15, 16, 18, and 19.

133. Active and Passive Voices

The sentences written in the active voice are numbers 1 and 4.

The sentences written in the passive voice are numbers 2, 3, and 5.

138. Making Your Mark with Sound-Alike Words

- (1) F
- (2) I
- (3) N
- (4) G
- (5) E
- (6) R
- (7) P
- (8) R
- (9) I
- (10) N
- (11) T
- (12) I
- (13) N
- (14) G
- (15) S

The fifteen-letter word is <u>fingerprintings</u>.

139. Regular Comparison of Adjectives and Adverbs

(1) smartest   (2) nicest   (3) bright   (4) smoother   (5) longest

140. Irregular Comparison of Adjectives and Adverbs

(1) most/least frightened

(2) more/less rigorous

(3) happier

Section Three: Mechanics

142. Working with Periods, Question Marks, and Exclamation Marks

(1) Can you remember your previous four phone numbers, Kyle?

(2) "I wish that this test was already over," John Smithers said.

(3) Sheryl asked, "Have any of these chickens crossed the road yet?"

(4) Great! You can see that these are the winning lottery numbers.

(5) Should these plants be moved into the shed for the season?

(6) Jackson exclaimed, "This party is absolutely terrific!"

(7) Did Anne say, "My coat is in the auditorium"?

(8) What is that extremely annoying sound?

(9) Please take that book to the bookmobile, Chauncey.

(10) Let's see what surprise the workers have in store for us.

(11) "Was John Lewis with you during the experiment?" the professor asked her assistant.

(12) Tell all of them to get down here immediately—or else!

Answer Key

⑬ Please call the housekeeper when you get a chance.

⑭ The office manager asked his maintenance official, "When will you be able to have your workers wash these windows?"

⑮ "Did William Shakespeare, the renowned playwright, really write all of those plays, or did somebody else write some, or most, or all of them?" the English teacher asked her students.

148. Commas in Action

① Wendall would like to go fishing, but his father needs his help on the farm.

② If Julio had not corrected the error, he would have earned a lower grade.

③ Because Julianne studied diligently for the examination, she passed with flying colors.

④ The long, exhausting journey finally ended.

⑤ My dad met my mom for the first time on June 14, 1975.

⑥ Clara asked, "Are these your violin strings?"

⑦ The family members visited New Orleans, Detroit, Chicago, and Los Angeles.

⑧ "I moved from California to Utah last year," the salesman declared.

⑨ Dear Nicolina, (as the salutation of a friendly letter)

⑩ Smitty, will you please open that door for me?

⑪ Mr. Pryal, the esteemed English teacher, knows the lyrics of many old songs.

⑫ Our friends, who are good bowlers, will travel to Spain this fall.

⑬ Since you look younger than twenty-one years old, I will need to see some identification.

⑭ Within a few weeks after her interview, the movie actress purchased a home in Hollywood.

⑮ As a matter of fact, this is the way home.

⑯ Hector married Louanna on August 7, 2006.

⑰ Stunned by the powerful punch, the boxer retreated to his corner.

⑱ Needless to say, the Fourth of July celebration was joyous.

⑲ Sincerely, (as the closing of a letter)

⑳ Yes, this is the man I will marry next year.

149. Some More Commas in Action

1. After the initial stage of the project, the manager made three changes.
2. Your neighbor, who has three dogs in his backyard, is the local bank president.
3. Yours truly, (as the closing of a letter)
4. Well, you can probably get there by then.
5. Excited by the news, the cameraman sprinted to the scene.
6. Dearest Dad, (the salutation of a friendly letter)
7. Can you read the next paragraph, Rachel?
8. "This documentary is very informative," Roger told Ray.
9. To tell the truth, my sister already knows about your plan.
10. Because Eddie needs a ride, I volunteered to take him.
11. As soon as the song was played, the children began to sing and dance.
12. Yes, you should begin the game without me.
13. These dogs bark loudly, and those cats love to scurry around the house.
14. He lives in Richmond, Virginia.
15. Dan Marino, who quarterbacked the Miami Dolphins for years, was always a threat to pass for a touchdown.
16. Joyce, the Little League representative, has been volunteering for many seasons.
17. The skilled carpenter purchased nails, hammers, crowbars, and putty at the local hardware store.
18. Sincerely yours, (as the closing of a letter)
19. He was my first choice, but the committee members thought differently.
20. The meteorologist answered your brilliant, intriguing question.

150. Comma Matching Contest

1. C
2. F
3. I
4. B
5. A
6. J
7. E
8. G
9. H
10. D

151. The Apostrophe

A. Mary's pictures

B. John's sister-in-law's coat

C. Les's speech

D. Fred and Garrett's space

E. Demetrius' address

Answer Key

153. Working with Apostrophes

1. the woman's scarf
2. Helen's scarf
3. the women's scarves
4. the boy's bike
5. Chris's bike
6. the boys' bikes
7. the baby's room
8. the babies' room
9. everybody's opinions
10. my uncle's ideas
11. someone's backpack
12. my brother-in-law's home
13. Jim and Nicole's car
14. Nicole's and Jim's cars
15. this month's magazine

154. The Colon

A. Please bring the following items with you: watch, ring, cell phone, and pen.

B. Dear Madam: (as the salutation of a business letter)

C. The following students have been selected for the varsity debate team: Matthew, Hillary, and Sophia.

D. My grandfather saw the movie *Superman*: *The Movie* in 1979.

E. Were you at the site at 4:40 that afternoon?

156. Colons and Semicolons in Context

1. Harriet loved to go to the shore; her brother really enjoyed going with her.

2. The boater was speeding around the lake for two hours; in fact, he was starting to annoy the people on the beach.

3. My great-grandfather's favorite movies include the following: *Vacation*, starring Chevy Chase; *One Flew Over the Cuckoo's Nest*, starring Jack Nicholson; and *Funny Girl*, starring Barbra Streisand.

4. Our fitness instructor recommends these healthy foods: carrots, peanuts, apples, grapes, and celery.

5. Let us plan to meet at 1:10 on the train platform.

6. (The secretary started her business letter with these words)

    Dear General McNamee:

    We would like to invite you ...

7. The author told the audience members that she plans to entitle her next book *Surfing: A Sport Like No Others*.

8. Our tour guide offered the group trips to these places: Juneau, the capital of Alaska; St. Louis, the Gateway to the West; and San Francisco, the City by the Bay.

9. We need to reach our goal of $10,000 in two weeks; therefore, we will step up our phone campaign starting tomorrow.

10. The nurse spent much time with that one patient; as a result, her time spent with the next few patients will be reduced.

162. All Sorts of Punctuation Problems

1. "Will you please hand me that wrench?" asked Jimmy Bevy.

2. She replied, "You can contribute any amount that you can afford. We accept all donations."

3. "They will find," Rex went on, "that this meal is very tasty."

4. The rancher said to her assistants, "We need to move this herd before the storm arrives. Let's get to it immediately."

5. "We swam thirty laps yesterday," Ricardo stated. "We will swim an additional twenty laps this morning."

6. "I have never met a man," Nicky said, "whom I respected more."

7. "Look out! Here comes that vicious dog," Mr. Boyle warned his children.

8. Did Ms. Wright say, "Yvonne can do no wrong"?

9. Laverne screamed, "You're going to knock over that expensive vase, Betty!"

10. "Can you take this heavy package to Tom?" Ted asked Tim. "You will need your car to haul it."

163. All the Punctuation Is Missing

(These are possible answers. There may be others that are acceptable.)

1. "Have you seen *Rocky* featuring Sylvester Stallone?" Lucy asked Malik.

2. There are several genres of literature that we will study here in college this semester: (1) short stories, (2) novels, (3) poems, and (4) plays.

3. The year Alfredo was born (1996) was the same year that his dad graduated from medical school.

4. Many subjects (physics, English, civics ...) challenge students to work diligently.

5. These mummies have been in the museum for many years; in fact, they have been here since the museum's inception.

⑥ Please bring these items to the work site this morning: hammer, chisel, drill, and saw. (The comma after <u>drill</u> is optional.)

⑦ Miguel's hat was found near the mall's main office.

⑧ "May I ask your sister-in-law to dance?" Ronaldo asked Paula.

⑨ "I—um—think that—well—you can come with us," the shy manager informed Rita.

⑩ "The conventioneers told of their 1967 [actually 1968] experiences in Chicago that summer," the assistant professor informed her students.

167. Capitalize These (Part One)

① Mike's cousin lives in Norwood, Massachusetts.

② Will the Pittsburgh Penguins play the New York Rangers this month?

③ Is 242 Northfield Ave. the correct address?

④ We studied about the Pacific Ocean on Wednesday and the Atlantic Ocean on Friday.

⑤ US 10 runs through Minnesota.

⑥ Which is your sign—Pisces or Libra?

⑦ Hank Hall joined the Boy Scouts of America in November.

⑧ When will the members of the United States Senate reconvene?

⑨ Gino's Pizza Palace is in the next town.

⑩ When was the Empire State Building opened?

⑪ How many Oscars has Meryl Streep won?

⑫ Three hundred guests attended the gala Labor Day event thrown by Uncle Joe.

⑬ John and Mary, two Americans, owned Wakefield Beverage.

⑭ Have you received your notes on Protestantism and Judaism?

⑮ Charles Lindbergh piloted *The Spirit of St. Louis* from New York to Paris in 1927.

168. Capitalize These (Part Two)

① My relatives, Uncle Ted and Aunt Flo, traveled in a Boeing airplane last fall.

② You will be intrigued by the movie *Murder on the Orient Express*.

③ The Statue of Liberty is a symbol of freedom.

④ The Bible and the Koran are popular books.

⑤ Miguel owns a Toyota Venza and a Nissan Ultima.

⑥ *Pride and Prejudice*, *Jane Eyre*, and *One Flew over the Cuckoo's Nest* are among Herb's favorite novels.

⑦ Mathematics, social studies, French, and English were hard classes for Juliet.

⑧ We purchased tickets for two Broadway musicals, *Jersey Boys* and *Billy Elliot*.

⑨ Chapter One, "How to Be a Success," is very well written.

⑩ This month we will read and discuss three short stories—"The Gift of the Magi," "The Necklace," and "The Open Window."

⑪ Have you seen Vincent Van Gogh's painting "Starry Night," or Edward Hopper's painting "Nighthawks"?

⑫ One of Lisa's favorite films is *Citizen Kane*.

⑬ My sisters especially enjoy two comic strips, "Archie" and "Family Circle."

⑭ Aunt Gina and Grandpa Gino visited the Grand Canyon last October.

⑮ Yvonne attended Cornell University in Ithaca, New York.

170. Spell It Right—And Win the Battle

The correctly spelled words spell the twenty-letter word *counterrevolutionary*.

Section Four: Show What You Know

171. Where Did All the Letters Go?

1. mileage
2. irregular
3. column
4. accommodate
5. height
6. unnecessary
7. villain
8. neighbor
9. regrettable
10. occurrence
11. seize
12. occasion
13. thorough
14. paradigm
15. nickel
16. miniscule
17. manageable
18. thief
19. parallel
20. cemetery
21. amateur
22. acquire
23. heiress
24. existence
25. believe
26. wield
27. weird
28. sergeant
29. prejudice
30. conscious
31. apparent
32. mortgage
33. condemn
34. grammar
35. calendar
36. benefit
37. genuine
38. license
39. discipline
40. foreign

172. Grammar and Twenty Thousand Leagues Under the Sea

1. was marked, has forgotten
2. adverb
3. These are items in a series.
4. The adjectives are *bizarre*, *unexplained*, and *inexplicable*.
5. those
6. adjective
7. that professional seamen were especially alarmed

173. Grammar, Mechanics, and Alice in Wonderland

1. Alice
2. and
3. adverb phrase
4. to do
5. had peeped
6. adverb
7. but, or, and
8. noun
9. The comma separates the speaker's exact words from the other parts of that sentence.
10. The quotation is a question.

174. Phrases, Clauses, and Sentences Found in "One Thousand Dollars"

1. past tense
2. adverb
3. complex
4. as
5. of new fifty-dollar notes
6. explained
7. simple
8. complex
9. would have been
10. fellow

175. Find the Mistake

1. A
2. A
3. B
4. B
5. A
6. A
7. B
8. A
9. C
10. C

176. Five Questions in Five Minutes (Parts of Speech, Phrases, and Clauses)

① conjunction

② If a pronoun is only replacing the name of a person, place, thing, or idea, it is simply a pronoun. If a pronoun describes a person, place, thing, or idea, it is a pronoun-adjective.

> *This* is fun. (pronoun only)
>
> *This* cat is lost. (pronoun-adjective)

③ The toys *on the stairs* were in Nina's way. (adjective phrase)
Nina fell *on the stairs*. (adverb phrase)

④ adjective clause

⑤ *Down* can be a noun, verb, adjective, adverb, or verb. Thus, it can be five different parts of speech.

177. Five Questions in Five Minutes (Sentences and Usage)

① b   **②** c   **③** b   **④** b   **⑤** b, c, e, f, i, and j

178. Five Questions in Five Minutes (Mechanics)

① a, b, c, d, and e   **③** a and b   **⑤** a, b, and c

② a, c, d, and e   **④** c and d

179. Five Questions in Five Minutes (Verbals and Subject Complements)

① a   **②** b   **③** c   **④** b   **⑤** b

180. Five Questions in Five Minutes (Confusing and Sound-Alike Words)

① quite: The fans were <u>quite</u> excited after their team's victory.
quiet: We should be <u>quiet</u> during the ceremony.

② weather

③ Yes

④ effect

⑤ cite: The experienced lawyer chose to <u>cite</u> several related cases during the trial.
site: The restaurant will be located on this <u>site</u> near the library.

Answer Key

NOTES

NOTES

NOTES

NOTES

NOTES

NOTES